A COURT REPORTER'S

NIGHTMARE

SUSIE KING LUTHY

Oct 14, 2015

Diane;
    Thank you for coming to my Book Club, you are so special to me.

I love you,
Susie

I would like to dedicate this book to my beloved late husband, Brent, and my wonderful son and daughter, Scott and Shauna.

I owe special gratitude to my three granddaughters, Brianna Dawn McElhannon, Editor; Brittany Sue Owens and Brenna Sue Luthy who have offered me untold aid, comfort and affection!

ACKNOWLEDGMENTS

I would like to thank the following people who were willing to read my novel and who gave me valuable advice and encouragement:

Myrtis Kendrick
Elayne Clark
Bonnie Robinson
Elaine Naylor
Barbara Cramer
Claudia Larsen
Carolyn Waggoner

CHAPTER 1

I backed out of my driveway in my new Ford Mustang Convertible heading for the Jefferson County Courthouse in Golden, Colorado, a beautiful small historic town located in the foothills west of Denver, Colorado. I am the Grand Jury Court Reporter and have been for five years. A new case is beginning before the Grand Jury Members this evening.

Darn, I wish my thoughts would stop haunting me. I am overly concerned about how much I keep dwelling on the past. My life drastically changed when Todd abruptly walked out of my life. I will never understand why. When he returned from his mission in Brazil, he did not try to contact me to explain why he no longer wanted a relationship with me. What was I supposed to think?

Needless to say, I was shattered by Todd's rejection. I loved him deeply and I thought he loved me deeply as well. Let's see, I hope I haven't forgotten anything; writer, computer, extension cords.

Gosh, I am exhausted. The mirror is definitely telling me no lies. I look horrible. I'm not getting enough sleep. I feel like 100 years old instead of 26. I do wonder, after all this time, how Todd is getting along, but why should I? He broke my heart. I heard through the grapevine that Todd was an outstanding missionary. I have no doubt about that. I feel extraordinary pain when I think what a wonderful husband and father he would have been. I waited faithfully for him for two and one half years.

Admittedly, over time, I'm feeling much stronger, but to be truthful to myself, I'm concerned that I will never stop loving him. Without the Savior in my life, it is frightening to think where I would be today.

Wow, what a beautiful evening. The sunset is casting a myriad of colors cross the sky. It is magnificent. I marvel at the beauty of nature. God has given us so much to be thankful for.

CHAPTER 2

Thank goodness I have arrived with plenty of time to spare. Who is that watching me from the other side of the parking lot? Oh, no. It's the big time District Attorney, Vincent Pagglione, formerly big shot lawyer from New York City. Vinny, his associates call him. Oooh! I know that he is looking at me. He is coming my way. I've got to speak to him in a civil manner no matter how I feel towards him.

"Hi Allison. Can I help you carry your equipment in"?

"Thank you. I appreciate the offer."

"How are you, beautiful?"

"Pretty good. I know I am frowning. Smile. I can't help my feelings of dislike towards this creep."

"Hey, Allison. Good looking vehicle."

"Yeah. I am enjoying it."

"I want to know something, Allison. When are you going to go out with me? I'm wearing down from your refusals."

"Vincent, I've already told you several times that I'm in love with someone."

"Okay. Okay. When you decide to fall out of love, give me a call. Will you?"

"Sure thing." My thoughts are so hateful. Dream on, Pagglione. Oh, my muscles are tight, and I haven't even begun working.

When we entered the courthouse I followed Vincent Pagglione to the elevator, and we rode together in silence and walked into the courtroom, and Vincent flipped on the lights. I began setting up my equipment. We were alone.

"Thanks for your help, Vincent. With the computer and all, I am pretty loaded down."

"No problem. Anytime."

I am so irritated at Vincent Pagglione. I've been driving my new car for at least three months. Surely he must have seen me drive up in it or leave in it before now. Why all of a sudden the interest? Besides that, he seems extremely strange to me tonight. Oh, forget it. Don't get carried away. Please, concentrate on what you are doing. I need to get my realtime set up before the Grand Jurors arrive.

Pagglione was sitting at the Plaintiff's table in the front of the courtroom. He pulled out his files to review the new case that was going to take place this evening. He has been with the District Attorney's office going on nine years. There are those who detest him. He has the reputation of being arrogant and very demanding.

His beady eyes stare right through me. I wouldn't say he is good looking, although his .appearance is impeccable. Admittedly, I look at Vincent Pagglione with a critical eye. He never has a strand of hair out of place or a scuff on his shoes. Total perfection. I do not trust him. He is cunning. Even his manner of speech reaches the level of perfection, not even uttering an "a" when he is speaking.

The longer I work with him, the more difficult it is to be in his presence. He's too overbearing. He's so ambitious and aggressive.

I know for a fact that his family are wealthy bankers in New York City, and he has attended the best private schools in New York. He graduated from Yale High School and was accepted to several law schools in the nation. He chose the University of Colorado in Boulder and apparently did extremely well, both academically and socially.

At this point in his life, he has very good connections. He's 43 years old and has been through two divorces. One thing for sure, he's able to play the political game very well as far as his career is concerned. Everyone knows that he has political ambitions, and he is looking ahead to run for the Senate or for Congress.

It's time to begin. I'm ready. Everything seems to be in working order. I don't know why I have to be so neurotic about certain things, but I am.

Geez, Pagglione has been running in and out of the courtroom like a chicken with his head cut off. He seems to be more nervous than usual. He is type A to the max.

Oh, I hope we don't end up working later than midnight. I'm scheduled to take three days of depositions in the morning. I can hear the sound of rain. I pray the rain ends before the session is over. I do not like driving at night in the rain.

These Grand Jury members have been meeting together for the past seven months. They are all acquainted with one another and seem to get along relatively well together. I like this group extremely well. There are a lot of well-educated people on the panel.

During breaks we laugh and tell jokes. We enjoy light conversations, but I have to be extremely careful never to discuss any case that they have heard previously or that they will listen to now. It is my practice to avoid talking too much to any of them on a one-on-one basis. They are never to ask me questions regarding my opinion of a case.

I was appointed to be the Grand Jury Reporter by Chief Judge Zacharelli, and have been serving for six years. My realization from the beginning was what an overwhelming responsibility it is.

A panel of 12 jurors are selected to hear the cases. Usually after one year they will bring in a new jury panel. The time has to be extended if the jurors are working on a case and it has not been completed.

It is common knowledge that a new panel of jurors is not selected until a case is completed and an indictment is either rendered or a No True Bill, which means that the person is found Not Guilty. If an indictment has been returned, then the person will have to stand trial or try to plea bargain.

In a Grand Jury session the Chief District Attorney or Assistant District Attorney presides. No Judge is present. Only the presiding District Attorneys may be present along with a special investigator and other investigators, if any, and the Grand Jury panel and the Court Reporter.

A defense attorney can be present with his client during their testimony, but he or she cannot ask questions, nor can they say anything. They are to remain quiet and only sit as an observer without uttering a word.

A Grand Jury is a very powerful body. They are able to ask any questions that they want to of any witness, call any witnesses they wish to hear from and interrupt the proceedings at any time to ask the District Attorney questions. They can ask any question that comes to mind about pertinent information that they feel they need to at any given time. The Grand Jurors have a great deal of latitude in how they proceed with a case.

The Grand Jury sessions are secret and everyone understands the Secrecy Rule; that no information gathered during a session should be leaked out from the Grand Jurors or anyone else present. The Secrecy Rule protects everyone involved in the investigations, as well as everyone involved in pursuing the truth of the matter.

Vincent Pagglione and Jim McCallister are the Assistant District Attorneys who are handling the case and Morgan Summers is the lead investigator on the case.

Jim McCallister is 40 years old. He is five-feet eleven, stout, wears thick-rimmed glasses and is not exceptionally good looking, but he does have a terrific personality and makes everybody laugh and, unlike Vincent, is easy to talk to. He is very well liked by his peers.

Morgan Summers is average looking. Her hair is bobbed on top of her head, and her nose definitely is too large for her face. I feel that Morgan Summers is indifferent towards me. I can't figure out exactly why.   Sometimes I think she could be jealous, but then I realize that that is ridiculous.

CHAPTER 3

Vincent Pagglione opened the Grand Jury session by speaking to the jurors. "Members of the Jury, good evening. Thank you all for coming. The case you will be hearing this evening involves a 39 year-old television news reporter. Her name is Rita Clark."

I gasped. I was trying not to show any emotion but my thoughts were total astonishment. Rita Clark. Many people know who Rita Clark is. As a matter of fact, she is one of the most popular television news reporters in the Denver area. I watch her specials on Channel 8. Rita Clark has done some very interesting stories.

One of the stories that was talked about for many days involved the plight of the mentally ill. She told about how many of these people are lonely and have no one to turn to. She also explained the reasons why they, unfortunately, end up on the streets homeless, and I thought she showed compassion in telling the viewers that nobody really seemed to care about them. She explained how much of their time is spent in struggling to get enough to eat and find a place to sleep.

I mumbled to myself. Wow, what in the world would Rita Clark have done wrong to be brought before a Grand Jury. She is such an excellent television news reporter.

Vincent Pagglione continued.

"Members of the Grand Jury: Rita Clark has staged this story. In other words, she wanted to bring public awareness to the fact that people in the Denver metropolitan area are training Pit Bulls to fight viciously, in fact, fight to their deaths."

I thought to myself. I am confused. I've never even heard of the words, staging a story.

Vincent is speaking in a serious tone of voice.

"Rita Clark set up an area in the back yard of someone's residence in Lakewood, Colorado. She got ahold of three Pit Bulls and hired two professional videographers, John Barker and Sam Lucas, to come to the area and film the Pit Bulls being trained. She bought muzzles and paraphernalia for the dogs and had John Barker and Sam Lucas film the dogs being tortured as well as being taught to be killers. The videographers shot the different sequences that Rita Clark requested them to film. She was being filmed as well, reporting the horrific abuses that these Pit Bulls have to endure. Ms. Clark told the public on her television special about the people who were abusing these dogs in order to use them for entertainment, how they put them in fighting rings where people come to watch and bet on who will be the winner. The dog remaining alive, of course, is the winner. Betting on who will be the winner of the fight involves big money."

I can write verbatim everything that is being said and think about things at the same time, and I couldn't help but think that what Vincent is stating reminds me of the roosters, the cock fights that took place in the early 19th Century where the roosters would fight until one killed the other one, and bets were placed on who would win.

Vincent Pagglione continued: "Rita Clark has illegally staged this story. No doubt about it. She was breaking the law as to how she went about preparing the story to be told to the public."

I sighed. I'm somewhat stunned by this investigation. To me it is like, so what? This is a crime? Don't most reporters have to set up situations and video the scenario, or whatever, to get a story? I thought that's what reporters did. Well, maybe there is more to it than it seems. Honestly, I thought I had heard everything.

As I write verbatim, I have to make sure that every word I hear is taken down, and if a word or words are not heard by me, I will politely interrupt the proceedings and ask Vincent Pagglione or a witness or a Grand Juror to repeat what they said, but it is a rarity to have to interrupt Vincent because he is extremely articulate.

It is an awesome responsibility to write down every word spoken. I have been trained to understand the importance of asking that something be repeated or to ask someone to speak up when I am not sure of what is being said. I do not like to interrupt very often, but then I also know that I better be capable enough to be able to take verbatim everything being said without too much interruption. Interrupt only when necessary is my motto.

This is one of the reasons for the rigorous training at the Academy and one of the reasons that I did not begin my career as a Court Reporter until I felt I had adequate knowledge of the English language, medical terminology, legal terminology,

English for Court Reporters. All of these subjects I took seriously.

I knew I could never stop training. I realized early on that I needed to read constantly which helped build my vocabulary. I always had a dictionary on hand. Our instructors were adamant about students being up-to-date on current affairs.

Court Reporting is a very demanding profession. It involves 100 percent concentration. When I have judges, attorneys, or witnesses on the stand who have heavy accents or garble their words, I get agitated. I am very aware of my responsibility to speak up and tell them that I do not understand what they are saying. On occasion I have asked for an interpreter in order to make sure that the record is as accurate as possible.

My background consists of studying Gregg Shorthand in High School, and I was an excellent typist as well. In fact, I received the Best Typist Award from Ogden High School in my senior year. My Court Reporting training was at Mile High Court Reporting Academy in Denver.

Vincent Pagglione continued:

"Members of the Grand Jury. This investigation is going to involve a lengthy period of time in that there are a long list of witnesses who will be testifying regarding this case. We will be calling Rita Clark to testify, maybe even as early as next week which will be the last week of May."

Now Jim McCallister, the Assistant District Attorney, has stood and is explaining in more detail the events that took place up to this point which made it necessary to initiate an investigation into the alleged illegal activities of Rita Clark as well as the videographers. After discussing some of the preliminary facts in the matter, Jim McCallister stated:

"We will begin testimony at the next Tuesday evening session. Morgan Summers, the lead investigator, will be the first to testify as to the events that took place in leading up to this investigation. Members of the Jury, we are going to release you early this evening, but many of the sessions are going to involve late nights, possibly even going into the early morning hours. Okay. Thank you for coming. You are excused. It is 9:00 p.m. We will reconvene next Tuesday evening."

CHAPTER 4

I am so relieved to be able to leave early. I want to get home in time to listen to the ten o'clock news to see if there will be anything said about the Grand Jury case and the charges filed against Rita Clark and the videographers, John Barker and Sam Lucas. I also have a rush transcript that has to be delivered by Thursday morning at the latest, and I need to get up early in the morning to work on the transcript before I leave by 9:30 a.m. to get to Denver to take a deposition at 10:30 a.m.

My head is swimming. Oh no, what does Vincent Pagglione want?

"Allison I need to let you know that more than likely this case will be ongoing for some time, and we are going to need all the transcripts on a rush basis. In fact, this case may go on until Thanksgiving or beyond. I hope you haven't made plans, because we don't want substitute Court Reporters in this case. We need you to be here every session for continuity."

"Yes, Vincent. From what I heard tonight, it sounds like a lot of working overtime. That's fine."

I am trying to hide my true feelings. I do not want to shout out loud what I am thinking, such as, what case? Please. There has to be something more to this case than what we all heard tonight. Maybe down the line we will hear that Rita Clark murdered somebody or is selling drugs. They probably just forgot to tell us. This case reminds me of that old woman on the Wendy's commercial that asks, "Where's the beef?"

Pagglione is a bozo. I wish I could say that straight to his face, but I don't have the nerve. I am so aggravated. Most certainly I have made plans for Thanksgiving. In fact, I am invited to go skiing in Park City for a week with Sarah, one of my best friends from Ogden, Utah who I grew up with. We planned to spend time with my family as well.

Sarah has spent a good deal of time making all the arrangements. We both love to ski and hike. We decided if the snow wasn't good enough at that time of the year, so what. We will go hiking with the family in the beautiful mountains surrounding Park City.

Nature is my companion. It is where I feel closest to God and His creations.

I feel an urgent need to get out of the sight of Vincent Pagglione. I don't want to say anything that I might regret later on. Besides I need to get home quickly to check the news and then go to bed so that I will be well rested for the big week coming up.

Vincent Pagglione is becoming such a pain. He does have an obnoxious way about him, the way he swaggers into the courtroom; the way he treats other people. He is arrogant beyond words, and he thinks he can do no wrong. Modesty definitely is not a part of his vocabulary.

Well, I better select my words carefully and call it quits for the evening. "All rush transcripts? Well, you know Vincent I haven't been charging you rush on the transcripts that I have been delivering to you rush. I'll have to get another Court Reporter to help me take some of the depositions I have booked, and I'll have to charge you rush on the transcripts. I have been spoiling you guys as far as my rates go."

Oh, no; my voice was shaking. I'm not thrilled about rushes all summer, and I have some excellent deposition work booked. Face it, the Grand Jury work is really my bread and butter. No matter how I feel, I have to go the extra mile and accommodate the District Attorneys.

As time passes, I'm beginning to feel about this guy the way others do. His demeanor has such a rough edge, and he doesn't look me straight in the eye when he is talking to me. He is definitely not a lovable type of guy. Oh well, I'll give him assurance that he can depend on me.

"Sure, Vincent. I'll do everything I can to get the transcripts delivered to you as quickly as possible. It sounds like a very busy summer."

"That it is, Allison."

Good Heavens, I don't dare tell him I have made other plans. I'm not looking forward to burning midnight oil all summer long. It's time to pack up my equipment and make sure that I have everything. I'm anxious to get on the elevator and out the door before Vincent shows up and follows me.

Oh, no. Here comes Rosie, one of the Grand Jurors. Rosie came running up and nervously blurted out, "Allison, I need to talk to you about something. Would it be possible for you to meet me down at Liberty Cafe? We could grab a private table."

You have got to be kidding, I thought. I can't believe this woman is for real. "Well, Rosie, you understand the Secrecy

Oath, don't you? To be honest, I'm surprised that you would ask me to talk to you in private. Impossible. That is out of the question and you know it as well as I do. If you do not walk away this instant, I will have to report you to the District Attorney's Office." Rosie stared at me and walked away without another word.

I am so furious at that woman. She should know better. I wonder what she is up to. I stepped into the elevator. Needless to say, I feel strangely violated. This has never happened to me before. In the six years that I have been the Grand Jury Court Reporter, nobody has ever approached me like that.

Well, I better try to forget it and keep my mouth shut. In the future I will make every effort to avoid her. The elevator door opened and as I stepped out and walked toward the entrance, Rosie suddenly appeared from out of nowhere and with tears in her eyes, she said: "Please don't feel offended by me approaching you. I would like to apologize. I meant no harm to you. I wanted to just be your friend and tell you something that I overheard someone saying about you. That's all. Anyway, I understand your position as well as my own. I am very aware of the Secrecy Oath that all of us are bound by. Let's just forget it, okay"?

I am astonished that she said she wanted to be my friend. I have to be polite to her, and I said, "I don't know about us being friends, Rosie, but, of course, we can talk about the weather or something that doesn't involve anything to do with the investigation of the case that we are about to hear. If we keep it on that level, nobody will get hurt. Do you understand"?

"Yes, I do. I certainly do. By the way, Allison, if I might say this to you. I certainly admire what you do. I can't believe that anybody can write down all those words accurately. All of the Grand Jury members feel the same way as I do. We all marvel at your poise and at your ability to be able to write down every word as you do and read back so confidently."

"Thank you for the compliment. Now, I need to go." I moved quickly to distance myself from Ms. Nosey. Rosie walked at a fast pace towards her car which was parked in a different direction than mine. Thank goodness. Then she shouted, "See you next week." I attempted to give her a friendly wave. Rosie smiled and waved back.

Finally I am rid of Rosie. I hope that is the last encounter with her. Where are my keys? I can't even think I am so distraught over that big fat Rosie. What is she up to anyway? What does she mean by the word "friend"? Rosie knows that is impossible. I better watch out. She is a troublemaker.

I am annoyed that she approached me. Well, I know that is a warning sign to be more cautious. As if I don't have enough to think about. I'm extremely tired and need to get some rest. The encounter with Rosie has stressed me out. Then, on top of that, I keep going back to the past, about how my life would have been so different if it hadn't been for Todd. Sometimes I feel like a broken record, but since I was a little girl, I always looked forward to being married in the temple and having a family. That is all I really wanted in life. I cannot understand how Todd could have been so attentive and loving towards me, always buying me lovely gifts on special occasions, writing me precious love notes while he was on his mission and then dropping me cold when he returned. It makes no sense to me or any members of my family. I have saved the love notes. For whatever reason, I'm not even sure of anymore.

We were high school sweethearts. Even when he left on his mission to Brazil, I wondered how I could possibly be able to get along without him while he was away.

I think back to the time I left Utah to attend Mile High Court Reporting Academy here in Colorado. I would like to, more than anything in this world, block out certain events that took place while I was attending the Academy. I would like to block them out of my mind forever, but I'm afraid that is never going to happen.

CHAPTER 5

In my second year at Mile High Court Reporting Academy, I was devastated by the brutal murders of Leo Davis, the owner and my teacher at the Academy. His wife, Annie Davis, was also murdered. She was pregnant.

When Leo Davis had not shown up for class on a Thursday morning, one of the teachers, George Newton, called the Davis's home, and when there was no answer George thought he better go over to Leo's home to check things out. When George Newton got to the Davis's, he rang the doorbell several times with no answer. Things began to seem very suspicious to him. He knocked loudly on the front door and the back door with no response from inside. Finally, George took it upon himself to take the key from a hiding place that he knew about and proceeded to enter the house.

Much to George's horror, the house was torn to pieces, and he found the bodies of Leo and Annie Davis in the bedroom. It was a terrifying and gruesome scene, one that George never talked about with anyone.

George called 911 immediately and when the District Attorneys and Detectives and the Sheriff of Jefferson County arrived, George told them in detail what had happened up to the time that he had called them.

George had to be hospitalized after the experience of finding Leo and Annie Davis dead. He was put on sedatives, and was never really the same happy-go-lucky person who everyone loved.

A search began, and it wasn't long before two suspects were taken in to custody. They were two men in their 20's who were former students who had attended the Academy. Leo Davis had to ask them to leave the school because they were being disruptive and showing disinterest in the curriculum. They were very rude and obnoxious toward both Leo and Annie Davis.

The two men were charged with the murders. Fingerprints were all over Leo Davis's home that linked them to the murders. The trial lasted six weeks. Ginger, my friend, and I would not go near the courthouse. It was too painful for us.

The two men were convicted of First Degree Murder and sentenced to life without parole in the Colorado State Penitentiary.

Ginger, who was one of my best friends from Mile High Court Reporting Academy, as well as myself, had a great deal of difficulty focusing on our studies after the murders of Leo Davis, our beloved friend and teacher, and his wife who was a wonderful person. Most of the students were also in limbo and mourning over their deaths.

In order for any of us to keep going, we had to keep telling ourselves that Leo Davis would have wanted us to continue onward and to be successful. We all knew that it would have made him happy because he was the type of gentleman who genuinely cared. Leo Davis never really cared about money. The school was never profitable. What he cared about most were his students, watching them progress.

I can still visualize the twinkle in his beautiful blue eyes when one of us achieved a higher speed. He wanted all of us to succeed. The dropout rate was so high at most Court Reporting Colleges that those left to carry on the torch was what made him desire to be such an outstanding teacher.

Leo Davis, had received the Diamond Award for being one of the best writers of Gregg Shorthand in the country. He was highly respected on a national level.

The Academy was closed for a week after the murders so that all the Davis family, friends and students could attend the funeral. I will never forget how saddened Ginger and I were during the funeral services. I can cry just thinking about how wonderful Leo Davis was to me. He always bragged about me in the other classes, telling the students that I had a special gift. He had a way of making all of his students feel special.

If it had not have been for Leo Davis and his encouragement, I'm convinced that I never would have completed the Court Reporting program. He was like a beacon of light, urging me on. I loved him and I know Ginger did too.

I am finally home. Brewster, our security guard, is smiling and waving me through. Brewster is a great security guard. He gives me a feeling of safety. Knowing that we have 24-hour security guards on duty is a plus. Thank goodness that we have a seven foot fence that goes all the way around the property.

I'm looking forward to getting in my hot tub and relaxing for a few minutes before I go to bed. When I arrived home, I threw my clothes on the chair, hurriedly put my swimsuit on, opened up the glass doors from the great room and stepped onto my private deck.

I immersed myself in the hot tub. It feels so good and the evening is delightful. I cannot stay very long. I want to take the time to read my scriptures.

I do feel blessed to have this lovely townhome. I enjoy the beautiful view of the City as well as the foothills. I enjoy the moss rock fireplace at the far end of the great room. It lends itself to a comfy atmosphere. Above the fireplace is a unique oak mantel where I placed some of my memorabilia and several pictures of my family.

Well, I better get out of the hot tub and check my messages. Mother has left a message that she needs to talk to me as soon as possible. She has something very important to tell me. That worries me.

I love talking to my mother. No one in this world could ever replace the love that I feel for her. She is always there for me, through the good times and the bad times. She is the center of my universe.

She calls me Allie. That is my nickname.

"Hi mother. Your message alarmed me. What do you have to tell me that is so important?"

"Allie, I'm not sure how to put this without upsetting you, but Lydia has to be put to bed for the rest of her pregnancy. Of course, being diagnosed with diabetes doesn't help the situation. She's having a very difficult time right now."

"Mother, I'm heartsick about Lydia having diabetes. I truly wish I had the time to come home and help her, but we are starting a new case in Grand Jury, and I will be totally involved until the end of summer and possibly up to Thanksgiving. I love my sister so much. I would prefer to be there helping her with the children than what I'm obligated to have to do."

"I know sweetheart. Your daddy and I will help her as much as we can. Lydia understands that you can't leave your responsibilities, but I know she would love to have you come home when you are able to. You are such a comfort to her. It is wonderful that you are so close and always have been.

I am very concerned about her health. David is beside himself with worry. He has so many irons in the fire that it seems -- Allie, wait just a minute. Honey, I'll call you tomorrow. Lydia is on the other line. I'll tell her we touched base and that you will come home as soon as you can get away. We all love you so much and daddy sends his love. He's hanging on every word as I'm talking to you. Take good care of yourself."

"Okay, mother. Tell Lydia that she is always in my prayers. Bye-bye."

I am so fortunate to have such a wonderful mother. My daddy has always given me a lot of attention and love as well. I can't bear to think that I'm not able to be with the family and especially Lydia during her time of need, but it is comforting to know that mother and daddy will be there to help her.

Lydia has helped me all through my life. She has been there when I needed her most, especially right after Todd crushed my heart. She rooted me on when I was a cheerleader in

Junior High School and at Ogden High School. Every award I ever received, Lydia was there to praise me.

I'll never forget when she married David in the temple. We stood on the steps of the temple afterwards taking family pictures. She was so beautiful and still is. I wanted more than anything else in this world to follow in Lydia's footsteps. Now, my sweet sister is needing me. This is her sixth child and probably will be the last with her health problems. It seems to me she seems as excited as if it was her first.

I've never known anyone to be so loving towards all of her children. I know the Lord will bless her with a healthy child. I know she will be alright. She has to be alright.

Time for bed. I have a nightly ritual of reading my scriptures and then saying my prayers. I feel so lonely without my family, and this ritual seems to have a calming effect on me.

The phone is ringing. It is late for someone to be calling. I will let them leave me a message. I better check and see who called.

"Allison, hello. This is Vincent. Sorry to be calling so late, but I didn't get out of the courthouse until 30 minutes ago. I know you will be not be happy to hear this, but we need the transcript from tonight's session rush. Hope you don't mind. I need it on my desk by 9:00 Thursday morning. Of course, charge us rush and if you would, please leave a message at the D.A.'s office telling me that you received this message. As usual, we always know we can count on you. Thanks."

Oh my gosh, I'm scheduled for depositions on a big divorce case in the morning that could very easily go through Friday. Well, the transcript that Vincent wants isn't that long. I will get up at 3:30 in the morning and begin preparing. I better set the alarm. I can hardly keep my eyes open.

I cannot believe the alarm clock is ringing already. It is 3:30 a.m. It is so tempting to shut it off and roll over and go back to sleep. Forget that notion. I have to get up and go to work. Vincent needs this transcript rush.

CHAPTER 6

I know that I'm turning into a regular workaholic. Some brewed herbal tea with fresh lemon sounds so delicious right now. I am going to prepare that and then get to work. Thankfully I have an office here at home. If I begin now, it should only take me a couple of hours to complete this rush transcript.

I am finished and hungry at the same time. I think I will cook a poached egg, bacon and wheat toast. Man, it smells so good and is delicious.

Time to get ready and head for Denver. It's always a dilemma for me to decide what to wear. I think my light gray silk blouse and dark gray jacket and slacks would be suitable.

My hair is so thick and curly. I guess I will pull it back in a twist and wear my strand of real pearls and earrings. I look pretty good if I say so myself.

The phone is ringing. "Good morning. Allison speaking."

"Allie, hi."

"Sarah, how are you?"

Sarah Taylor is my best friend, and I can trust her in every way. We have grown up together and know each other inside and out. I always feel extremely comfortable in telling her personal things, knowing it will not be spread around. Sarah also has helped me through some very difficult times, especially when Todd rejected me. I will always be indebted to her.

We have had some wonderful times together, such as regularly going to Lagoon, an amusement park, playing hooky from school just on one occasion, the fun things that teenage girls do but nothing too outlandish. We both understand where to draw the line.

Sarah responded, "Fine. I just wanted to check on you to make sure you are okay. If I don't have contact with you often, I start to worry about you."

"Worry does not do any of us any good, Sarah. Sometimes it is very difficult for me to remember that. By the way, mother called this morning and Lydia is having difficulty with her pregnancy."

"Oh no, Allie. Is there anything I can do to help?"

"You know, Sarah, Lydia being diagnosed with diabetes does not help matters. If you would drop in to see her once in a while, that would cheer her up. She feels comfortable around you. Lydia loves you Sarah. Of course, you know that.

I'm on the run. I've got to drop a Grand Jury transcript off at Meg's for proofing, and then I'm headed for Denver."

"Okay, Allie. Call me when you have got some time to talk. I'll be here after 8:30 tonight. You know, as far as I'm concerned, Allie, you are turning into a regular workaholic. No matter what, Allie, we are going on the family skiing trip to Park City. Don't forget that, and don't tell me you have too many transcripts to work on. If you are not careful, I'm going to think that money means more to you than friendships."

"You make me laugh. I am beginning to wonder myself. Sarah, if I turn down our Park City trip for work, The Stein

Ericksen Lodge, total luxury, then I need to have my head examined. Talk to you later."

I did not want to mention to Sarah that Vincent Pagglione does not want me to make any plans for quite a while, and that he needs me exclusively on this Rita Clark case. That seems strange to me. When I mentioned to Vincent at the first session that Ginger would help out if I needed to be away, he was adamant that I be there every session until the case is completed.

I have to move quickly. I need to get downtown Denver by 9:30. I am a fanatic about time. I always like to be at my destination at least one hour early to set up for a deposition. I like to be ready to go before any of the parties arrive. I tend to get extremely nervous if I run late. It is 7:30 a.m., which gives me plenty of time to get to Denver, park, and head for the Law Office.

I am taking this case for the law firm of Jones, Jones and Walton, which is a very prestigious firm that represents many wealthy clients. They work on a lot of high profile divorce cases. They have built quite a reputation for themselves and have just moved into plush new offices on 17th Street. When I worked in Federal Court on a big drug case, the lead attorney was Baxter Walton. The drug case went on for two weeks and the transcripts were ordered expedited. I had to work furiously to get the transcripts completed. Everything was ordered rush. They were very impressed with my professionalism and timeliness, and through the recommendation of Baxter Walton, the law firm has hired me to do their deposition work ever since. They verbalized that they thought I was an excellent Court Reporter, or so they told me.

I found a parking space a block away from the law offices which makes it handy to walk with my equipment on rollers. I entered the building and stepped into the elevator. When I reached the 16th Floor, the elevator opened up to a luxurious waiting area. Cindy, the receptionist, was sitting at the front desk.

"Hi Cindy. How are you today?"

"Hi Allison. I'm as good as can be expected. Let me take you to the conference room, and then I'll let Mr. Walton know that you have arrived."

The conference room is ornate. The walls are carved in deep cherry wood, and the furnishings are beautiful, especially the conference room cherry wood table. It is very impressive. The swivel chairs are dark rose with needlepoint eagles on the back of the executive chairs, and the views from the full length windows are spectacular. You can see the skyline of the Rockies.

I immediately began setting up my equipment. Mr. Walton stuck his head in and said, "Hi Allison. How have you been?"

"Great. How are you?"

Baxter Walton nodded and smiled. "Busy, but I'm hanging in there." Then he disappeared.

Baxter Walton is six-foot two. His hair is black with a tint of gray. I happen to think he is very handsome. He is fun to be around. His personality is more lighthearted than most attorneys, and he makes me laugh, especially when he tells jokes and laughs louder than anyone in the room. He's top notch as far as I'm concerned. It did not take long before the conference room filled with lawyers and paralegals.

Mr. Walton represents the Petitioner, Lily Monroe. Lily Monroe is a small woman with grayish hair. She has eyes that sparkle and a pug nose. Her silk dress and jewelry are exquisite.

Mason Black is the attorney for the Respondent, Ralph Monroe. Mr. Black is a large burly man with a mass of gray hair and a gray mustache which is clearly in need of care. Immediately upon receiving the necessary information from Mason Black, I knew that he was going to drive me crazy with his meek voice. Sometimes, I noticed from the beginning, it sounded like a squeak. I knew that I would have to keep telling Mason Black to speak up or repeat the question he had asked.

Ralph Monroe, Mason Black's client, looked like he had experienced a bit of the so-called good life. His face has the telltale signs of too much drinking, the red veiny look. He is definitely rugged looking, and appeared to be the kind of guy who did not like the idea of aging.

Ralph Monroe has blonde hair which is beginning to gray on the edges. He wears expensive sunglasses. His features are bold and he has a disingenuous smile. Most annoying to me initially was that he smiled a lot.

He is dressed to appear more youthful than his years, wearing a bright colorful shirt and khaki shorts, along with wearing a pair of name-brand sandals. His outfit is set off with lots of expensive jewelry, a gold necklace and diamond rings on most of his fingers. Ralph Monroe blurted out some of his personal history when Lily Monroe and the attorneys left the conference room for a brief period. He told us that he is now living in the Florida Keys part of the time. A portion of his time is spent in Denver and a portion of his time he spends in Paris. He tells us that the home in Paris is of enormous contention between him and his wife because they both want to take possession of that home. Sometimes I cannot help but want to laugh at how much we can complicate our lives.

Mason Black brought his paralegal, Kitty, who he repeatedly called Kitten. She came with him from Florida. Mr. Black bragged to us about how he passed his bar in three states, making him eligible to practice in Colorado, Florida, and New York.

I think Kitty is a very unusual looking woman. She is half the age of Mason Black. Her dark skin has, without a doubt, been overexposed to the sun. She has a knockout figure. She is not dressed like a professional but looks more like a hussy. Her makeup is overdone to the max and her hair is long, bleached white and bushy from being over-permed. Kitty's fingernails are fake and painted a bright cherry red, matching her red lipstick. She has on a pair of strapless red patent leather shoes accented by red nylons.

I notice that she talks nonstop when she gets the chance and is very chummy with Mason Black. She is anxious to grab one last cigarette before the depositions begin. Kitty is the most colorful person present. The funniest habit she has is she chews bubble gum, and when she returned to the conference room she popped a piece of gum in her mouth and began to blow small bubbles. It seemed to me that she was deliberately trying to irritate the attorneys.

I wrote down all of their names and who they represented. I already had been mailed a Notice of the case. So the caption of the case is in my possession. All of the introductions had taken place, and I gave the parties my business card.

When Mr. Walton came back into the conference room he said, "Allison, I need you to mark several exhibits before we begin. They are in the order we prefer."

"Yes, sir."

"Thank you Allison. Would you please swear in Mrs. Lily Monroe?"

"Mrs. Monroe, if you would please raise your right hand." Mrs. Lily Monroe squirmed in her chair and facing me, she slowly raised her right hand to be sworn in. "Do you solemnly swear that the testimony you are about to give in this case will be the truth, the whole truth, and nothing but the truth so help you God?" Slowly and carefully Mrs. Lily Monroe said, "I do."

I could feel the hateful vibes immediately when Mrs. Monroe's testimony began. In many of these circumstances, particularly in domestic cases, I feel like an intruder. In this situation, the air was putrid. There was so much anger and animosity in the room. Mr. and Mrs. Monroe were glancing over at each other with wicked eyes, and I knew that if either of them came unhinged, there would be trouble. I dread this type of atmosphere. I pray that things do not deteriorate to the point of violence. I have experienced violence before in some domestic cases. My immediate reaction is fear.

Mason Black, Ralph Monroe's attorney, called Lily Monroe for examination. Mason Black began speaking at a fast pace, around 300 words a minute, and I knew that this was going to be a very difficult day.

"Mrs. Monroe, do you mind if I call you Lily?"

"Lily is fine."

"Lily, first of all, would you please state your full name for the record."

"Lily Francis Monroe."

"And your present address?"

"Mr. Black, I need to speak to my attorney."

"Certainly. Lily, any time you would like to confer with your attorney, please do so. Also, if you need to take a break, let me know. Do not hesitate to tell me if you do not understand a question that I am asking. When you do answer a question, I will assume that you understood."

"Okay."

Mrs. Lily Monroe whispered in Mr. Walton's ear.

Mason Black glanced over at me and said, "We are back on the record. Would you like me to ask the question again, Mrs. Monroe?"

"No. That's fine." Then Lily Monroe continued:

"I own four homes; one in Aspen; one in the Florida Keys; one in Beverly Hills; and one in Paris. The home in Paris is my favorite, because I have done all the decorating myself. I love that home. Without bragging, I have done a beautiful job of putting the home in great shape. It sits on 20 beautiful acres of land outside of Paris. I am in Beverly Hills often but it varies, depending on my mood."

I shook my head. I think it is unbelievable that anyone could be so filthy rich. The testimony became very combative. Mrs. Monroe and Mr. Monroe brought in their massive collections of jewelry. It was displayed in one of the other conference rooms. If I didn't know what I was there for, I would have thought I was attending a jewelry sale. The diamonds are exquisite and of the highest grade. Both parties own an enormous amount of jewelry, although, no doubt about it, when Mr. Monroe talked about his antique cars, and showed us pictures, I couldn't believe it. He is in possession of over 100 automobiles, ranging from a Model T Ford, to a Rolls Royce and a fully restored 1955 two-seater Thunderbird worth thousands.

I couldn't help thinking: People can have too much. It boils down to greed and just plain selfishness.

The time is flying by. It is six o'clock, and they have finished deposing Lily Monroe. Mrs. Monroe seems badly shaken and on the verge of tears. Sensitive questions were asked regarding the length of her marriage to Mr. Monroe. You could tell from her demeanor, she was emotionally drained and visibly heartbroken.

I asked Mr. Walton, "Is it alright if I leave my equipment in the conference room for the night"?

"Sure thing. We lock up before we leave and it's safe."

"Thank you. Have a good evening."

"Thanks. You do the same, Allison." Mr. Walton flashed a friendly smile and left.

I am here by myself. I need to make sure the exhibits are in order and then I will check my messages. I'm starting to feel fatigue. I would rather take a First Degree Murder case than a domestic case. Worst of all is a custody case.

Well, I better check my messages. Oh, one from Vincent, one from mother, two calls from Sarah and one from the National Association of Court Reporters.

I think I will wait until I get home to return the calls.

Cindy is at the receptionist desk. "Cindy, see you in the morning. Have a nice evening."

"Yes, you too, Allison. Have a safe drive home."

"Thank you, Cindy. You do the same."

CHAPTER 7

On the way to my vehicle, I thought, what does Vincent Pagglione want now? I left a message at noon with the D.A.'s office to tell them that the rush transcript will be delivered tomorrow morning as they requested.

It seems unusual for Sarah to be calling me back twice. That's out of character for her to do so. I hope everything is alright with Lydia.

I know what the National Association is calling me about. They want to know if I would be interested in working on the realtime Committee next year, and I'm beginning to think that would be a wonderful opportunity for me to do that. I have decided that I'm definitely going to say yes.

Mother called me during the day. She knew that I would be in a deposition all day. Now that Lydia has been diagnosed with diabetes and pregnant, I feel worried that something may happen to her.

Allie, I muttered to myself, you have been subjected to the negative side of life too long, and you are looking for a disaster to come around the corner. In the line of work I'm in, it is understandable that sometimes life seems surreal. I will call mother the minute I get home.

I have to stop by Meg's house to pick up a transcript, and then I will swing by Dairy Queen and pick up a burger and herbal tea. It does not look like Meg is home. Bless her heart. She has left the transcript in an envelope in the milk box on the front porch. That was a good idea on her part. Meg is a funny gal. She bought the milk box for one reason only, to put the transcripts in.

Meg attended Mile High Court Reporting Academy at the same time that I did. I will never forget the look of disappointment on Meg's face when she told me that after six months of trying to reach the speed of 180 words a minute, she was going to have to quit. Her nerves were shot. Meg even looked me straight in my eyes and told how much she envied me for my natural abilities in being able to go from one speed to the next with no effort at all.

It is true that I was a natural, but I never bragged about it. I always tried to be tactful and quiet about being gifted, reaching higher speeds in very little time when it took most people so much longer.

Meg has many talents. In fact, she plays the violin beautifully. Two years previous she was selected to play with the Denver Symphony Orchestra as a regular. I am so thrilled that Meg wanted to proof for me. She is a perfectionist.

Everything is working out for both of us. We work as a team and we think a lot alike. I have decided to start using a modem to transfer the cases back and forth, and I will foot the bill for the equipment Meg needs. Our next step will definitely be to go on the internet. This will save us a lot of time. I'm beginning to realize that using every advanced technology possible will free me up so that I will have more time to do something else besides work, such as being with Lydia more often and go on more family outings in the beautiful mountains of Colorado and Utah and, in particular, hike.

My spirits elevate when I think about the many enjoyable experiences of camping trips with my family. Those are such wonderful memories. Oh, how I love nature. God created this magnificent earth for us to enjoy. I'll still never forget when my father let me catch a Rainbow Trout at the ripe old age of three. He taught me that if you catch the fish, you gut the fish. So, I gutted my fish and gutted many more fish thereafter. I learned a lesson from the experience for sure.

That makes me want to laugh. When I think about my daddy, all I can say about him is, he is such a dear man, a man for all seasons.

Home at last. Brewster is at the gate.

"Hi Brewster."

"Allison, Hi." With a huge grin on his face, Brewster shouted, "You are a ray of sunshine." He is such a wonderful guy.

I drove up to my townhome, parked my car in the garage and when I got inside I sighed a bit. First things first, I said out loud. I am starving. I will eat my burger first and then call mother. It is not the most nutritious choice for dinner, but I have so much to do that I don't have time to cook tonight. I am anxious to talk to mother about what is going on with Lydia. My love Lydia.

I know in my heart that nothing is wrong or mother would have left me a message. I pray through all of Lydia's health problems, she has a beautiful healthy baby. Sometimes, I have to admit, I feel jealous in ways of Lydia because she seems to have it all, a wonderful kindhearted husband who honors his priesthood and would do anything for her; five very polite and generous children, and they all love to attend church and study the scriptures together. David is the epitome of a loving father who puts his love of the Lord and his family first. Whenever his children need him for encouragement, or anything, he is always there for them.

When he bears his testimony, it comes from deep within. The last time I was in testimony meeting with my family, David bore such a strong testimony of the truthfulness of the gospel, and he is the first to tell all of us of the greatness of our prophet, Joseph Smith, and continues to remind us of how much Joseph Smith was persecuted and how much he sacrificed to bring about the restoration of the Church of Jesus Christ of Latter-day Saints.

The devotion that Lydia has to David is obvious. They work together as a team, and it is so lovely to observe their unconditional love for one another. Lydia never complains and yet she has had a toddler under foot for some years now. If I can be anywhere near what she is as a human being, I will know that my life has been well lived. The delivery of this baby has to be alright. I pray my sister will live long enough to raise her children.

I need to call mother.

"Mother, hi."

"Hi Allie. How are you?"

"Mother, I am fine, I guess. I got your message while I was downtown Denver taking a deposition, and I'm home now. How is Lydia?"

"Oh honey, she is going to be alright. She just needs to take it easy and eat right so she can carry the baby to full term. I will try to help her at least four times a week, and Mitch said he would go over to Lydia's house when he can and give her a hand. "Allie."

"Yes, mother."

"Something has happened that I think you are going to be happy about."

"What? Good news would be wonderful mother."

"Well, as you know, since Mitch has been home from his mission, he has dated several girls but none seemed to be the right one for him."

"I know what you are going to say, mother, before you say it."

"What, Allie?"

I started to giggle. "Mitch has met the girl of his dreams."

"Oh, Allie. You are always a step ahead of all of us."

"You know, honey, I might as well tell you the truth. I am not sure I should say this, but I don't think your daddy has been his normal self since you and Todd didn't end up together. That pretty much did us both in, but -- but "

"Mother, don't cry." I am glad mother cannot see me trying to hold back my tears. I fell silent for a moment. Then I lovingly said: "Well, I couldn't be more thrilled for my brother. He is so handsome and such a genuinely good person. For Heaven's Sake, he has been so good to me. No doubt about it, he is the best, and he deserves the best. Aren't you going to tell me who the lucky girl is, or are you going to just keep crying?"

"Well, Allie, we have just met her once. She has moved here from California. Her name is Gloria Johnson. Of course, she is a member of the church and sings beautifully. Both daddy and I like her a lot.

I know Mitch will want to fill you in on all the details."

"I can hear you, mother, still crying. Are you alright? Mother, I am so thrilled for Mitch. I cannot help it, but I still feel a lot of anger mixed with sorrow when Todd's name is mentioned."

"Allie, I am sorry to have even brought it up. What was I thinking? I love you so much and your dad and I hated to see you hurt so deeply. I pray you will continue -- wait a minute, Allie. I have a call coming in. I will be right back, honey. Honey, it's Lydia. She needs to know if I can watch the three younger ones tomorrow.

Look, don't worry about Lydia. She misses you terribly and wants to talk to you when you get a chance. She does understand that you are working under a lot of pressure right now, but she does want you to know that you are always in her prayers. I will call you tomorrow and let you know what is going on. Now, think positive. Everything turns out for the best in the end. I love you."

"I love you too."

I can't believe that Mitch is in love. I am so happy for him. How wonderful to meet someone that you adore. I truly wonder if I will ever meet someone that I loved as much as Todd. I've been on some pretty creepy dates since I've been here in Colorado. Sometimes it has left me in a depression that is very difficult to overcome. "Think positive," mother always tells me. She is definitely right. She always gives me tidbits of wisdom to live by, and she always lifts me spiritually.

I have got to call the D.A.'s office. I left a message for Vincent that I would get in touch with him as soon as possible, but first I want to talk to Sarah.

I hope she is home. "Sarah speaking."

"Sarah, you called me twice today. What are you doing"?

"Nothing earth shattering. I just thought you sounded lonesome last night, and I wanted to make sure that everything was alright. Actually, Allie, I'm not being completely honest with you. I still, down deep in my heart, feel tremendous fear that you might fall into a depression again. Allie, I know it is a touchy subject, but we all love you so much, and I know that you have made a remarkable recovery. You are even beginning to get back your sense of humor."

"Sarah, I am doing so much better with the help of my Heavenly Father, my family and good friends like you. Of course, I know I can always trust you to keep a secret. I guess it is a secret. Mother never really said that it was, but Mitch has met a girl that he likes a lot. She has moved here from California and mother and daddy said she's lovely."

"Great news, Allie. Mitch is a great guy. He is so wonderful. All the girls used to swoon over him. I certainly have never worried about Mitch. He's one person that has his feet on solid ground. He's so much like your father."

"He is, isn't he? He's been the dearest brother to me. Anyway, her name is Gloria Johnson. I can't wait to meet her. You may meet her before I do."

"Allie, I look forward to meeting her."

"Sarah, I have got to go now. Love you. I am grateful for one thing, your friendship over the years. Hopefully, if we live according to the Savior's teachings, we will be together with our families and friends like you eternally."

"Allie, beautifully said. That's a goal I'm constantly working toward, a promise I'll try to keep. Please, Allie, don't work too hard. It isn't worth it. I love you, and be good."

"I love you too. Take care."

I need to call Vincent. He is not answering. I will leave a message and tell him that I am returning his call. I do not want to burn bridges, but something about this case in Grand Jury smells like a rat.

CHAPTER 8

I arrived at the deposition, as usual, one hour early. Baxter Walton appeared in the conference room to greet me. "Hi Allison. Ready for another fun day?" He chuckled.

"Hi, Mr. Walton. I suppose I am. Do you need any exhibits marked before we begin today?"

"I do, Allison. Let me go retrieve those photos from my paralegal. Hey, what do you think of Kitten or should I say Kitty?"

I couldn't help but feel mischievous. "You have to admit, she certainly livens up the room. I especially like her red nylons and the red fingernail polish to match."

"Just between you and me, Allison, Mason Black seems to be robbing the cradel with this gal."

"I thought the same thing. He seems very proud of himself. What a bunch of characters." Baxter Walton began to laugh.

I laughed heartily with him and said, "Oh, Mr. Walton, you have such a good sense of humor. They say that you will live longer if laugh more often." Mr. Walton left the conference room and returned shortly.

"Allison, here are the photos I need marked."

"Yes, sir."

"Would you please mark these as well?"

"Sure. Wow, Mr. Walton, these photos of Mr. Monroe's antique automobiles are unbelievable. This Rolls Royce must be worth a fortune. Oh, and these photos of all the jewelry they own. I've never seen such a spectacular collection of diamonds."

"I know what you mean. Allison, some people just can't buy enough to satisfy their insatiable desires."

Kitty entered the room first, looking like a mannequin. She had on a tightfitting dance leotard, low in the front, enough to distract all the men in the room. Over the leotard she had a metallic miniskirt on, and her legs were covered with lacy black tights. She wore shoes with at least six inch heels.

I can't help but feel amused and thought, Boy oh boy, she sure can strut in those high heels. She asked me, "What is your name again?"

"Allison Smith."

"I just love the name Allison."

"Thank you, Kitty."

"Allison, would you mind showing me how you work that magic machine? What is it exactly that you do? It is so fascinating."

"I write brief forms which show up as letters on the machine. Here I will show you."

"Golly, Allison, you are unbelievable"

"This is called realtime, when you write on the court reporting machine and the English words come up on the computer. We, who can write realtime, have programed our own personal dictionaries."

"I swear, you are some kind of a magician. Awesome."

"Well, I wouldn't consider myself a magician, but thank you for your interest." I thought: Kitty is so nice and extremely funny. I like her.

Baxter Walton returned to the conference room and said, "We will be taking Mr. Monroe's deposition next." I couldn't help but be relieved that Mr. Monroe, no matter what anybody thinks of him, is articulate and speaks with confidence.

Mason Black, on the other hand, slurs his words. He has a strange accent that is very difficult to understand, and I am not the only one in the room that cannot understand him. I have had to ask him to repeat himself several times. At times he speaks so fast and swallows his words which is beyond irritating. I know everybody in the room looks at him with a question mark on their faces. Mason Black is oblivious to his poor manner of speech. Yesterday he gave me the look of death because I had to interrupt him several times to ask him to repeat what he had said.

The deposition began at l0:30 a.m. It turned out to be a grueling day for me. Baxter Walton fired the questions at Mr. Monroe, and Mr. Monroe, not being shy, fired the answers right back in an arrogant manner. Objection after objection went back and forth for the entire day. I had to read back several times, and by the end of the day I felt thoroughly exhausted. By 6:00 p.m. the deposition ended. Baxter Walton said: "That will be all." Relief was on his face when he said, "We do not need to return for a third day of testimony."

I also am relieved. "Okay," I asked, "Who would like copies of the transcripts"? All the attorneys ordered transcripts. They thanked me for my services, and then the parties quickly left the conference room, all except for Baxter Walton.

"Allison, as you can see from the testimony, Ralph Monroe has so much money that we are having difficulty tracking it down. There are millions of dollars that our expert accountants can't find. It's going to take several months before we can get to the bottom of this. After we find out how much he is worth, we may request a settlement conference."

Baxter Walton winked at me. "Thanks for coming. You know, you are our favorite Court Reporter."

"I appreciate you saying that. You are delightful to work with."

"Have a great weekend, Allison."

"You do the same, Mr. Walton."

"Feel free to use the phone or do what you need to do. The place is yours."

"Thanks. I need to check my messages."

"Like I said, the place is yours."

I packed up my equipment and reached for the phone. I better call Vincent Pagglione and see if, by chance, I can speak to him. I have the number that will get straight through to his office. "Hi Vincent. This is Allison. You called me. How can I help you?"

"Yes, Allison. I am glad you called. I was just leaving. We will be meeting twice a week at 7:00 sharp."

"Okay Sure. What evenings will we be meeting?"

"Starting next week, Tuesdays and Thursdays. Also, we received the Rita Clark transcript this morning. Thank you for the expedited delivery.

"You bet."

"Allison, I'm probably repeating myself, but we will need all of these Grand Jury transcripts rush. I know I had mentioned it before, but I thought I better confirm this request with you now so that you can plan for it. Will you be able to do that for us?"

I hesitated before I answered. "Yes. I plan to get some help from Ginger. She can take most of the depositions I have booked for the next six months."

"Great. Well, we will see you next Tuesday evening then. Thanks for returning my call."

"Okay. See you then."

I cannot believe how valuable Meg is. She has saved the day for me again. She is so dependable. She always meticulously proofs everything I give her. That gal is worth her weight in gold. I am going to give her a well-deserved raise. I think I'll call her right now and tell her.

"Meg, this is Allie. I wanted to thank you for being so helpful. You are a jewel. I am still downtown, but we finished the depositions. It got pretty tense at times, believe you me. I thought once or twice during these two days that Mr. and Mrs. Monroe were going to have an all-out war, but luckily it ended without any violence.

Anyway, I have been thinking about how much you have helped me out lately. I would like to give you a raise, and I am also going to include a bonus in your check for delivering that rush transcript to the D.A.'s office this morning. I hope the raise will help you out." "Wow. I appreciate a raise, Allie. I hope also that we will be working together for many years to come.

By the way, Allie, I have read all the instructions for the new modem, and we are in business. I will run you through the procedures when you get ready to send me the first part of that divorce case. Okay?"

"Okay, Meg. I can't thank you enough."

Before Meg started at Mile High Court Reporting Academy, she had received a Business Administration degree in English and was planning to get her Teaching Certificate. Through some encouragement from a boyfriend, she decided to study to become a Court Reporter instead.

The academic portion of the Court Reporting Program was a breeze for her. After practicing hour-after-hour every day to attain the speed of 180 words per minute, she still couldn't write at that speed with any clarity. So she decided to give it up and opened up a proofing and scoping business for Court Reporters.

"Meg, I have to go. I have to say that I think this new technology is fantastic. The modem is so much quicker, and it will save us a lot of running back and forth. As soon as I am ready to send this divorce case through to you, I will let you know, and you can walk me through the procedures. I will be talking to you probably on Sunday."

"Okay. See you Allie, and thanks again for giving me a raise. I can always use it."

"You deserve it girl. Talk to you later." Before I left the conference room and headed for home, I picked up Chinese food on Smithfield Avenue and got home in time to hurriedly eat, and then I called Lydia.

"Lydia, hi. How are you feeling?"

"Hi Allie. How is my favorite sister doing"?

"Lydia, I have been praying for you. I have faith that you are going to end up doing well, and you will have a healthy baby. I love you so much. You need to follow doctor's orders, and thank the Lord that mother and daddy are there to help you. Mitch will help you too. As much as the Relief Society sisters love you, you know that they will be there for you.

I wish I could be there to help you with the children, but I'm working long hours right now. I'm stuck in a Grand Jury case that is requiring a lot of rush transcripts."

"I know. Mother told me that you are under a lot of stress from too much work. Honey, don't you worry about me. I'll be fine. David gave me a blessing last night, and I feel better already.

Sarah visited me yesterday. Bless her heart. She brought the kids some of her baked goodies. What a wonderful friend Sarah has been to you, Allie."

"Oh, I know. Her kindness has been an example to me, that's for sure. She is so giving."

"Allie, I need to go. Sister Armstrong is coming by to bring me a bunch of books she thinks I might enjoy reading. I love you so much. Thanks for calling, and I understand the reason why we can't keep in touch more often. It is because of your busy schedule right now."

"Thank you for your understanding. I love you, Lydia. We'll make up for lost time. Tell the kids how much Aunt Allie loves them. I know that mother and daddy have put your name in the temple often. That has to be a great comfort to you."

"It definitely is. Hugs and kisses to you, Allie."

"The same to you."

I feel so much encouragement after talking to my sister. Lydia is so special. No matter what trial she is going through, she is always thinking of others and how she can serve them. She is spiritual and loves the Savior with all her heart. She constantly instills in me the desire to be a better person.

My mind is racing. I wish I could talk to Lydia or Sarah about this strange encounter with Rosie. I am worried about why Rosie approached me. Wanting to be my friend is certainly not true. She has disturbed my peace of mind. It just doesn't add up. I have always made it a practice when talking to the Grand Jury members to keep the conversation light and never get personal with them. I realize how important it is to be professional and to use a lot of discretion in what I say to any members of the Grand Jury. Why would Rosie have the nerve to approach me? I noticed she had tears in her eyes. The woman is up to no good. I need to avoid her at any rate.

My phone is ringing. "Hi, Allie. It's me."

"Sarah. Hey, thank you for visiting Lydia. You are so thoughtful."

"She is a trooper, that's for sure. Allie, her children are so sweet, not to mention well behaved."

"I know. Lydia puts her heart and soul into raising those kids in a righteous manner. Before they go to school in the morning, the family reads the scriptures for fifteen minutes, and then they all kneel in prayer. I dearly love those kids as if they were my own."

"That's understandable. They are adorable.

Allie, how did your day go?"

"To tell you the truth, Sarah, I had a difficult day. The attorney from Florida, Mason Black, is so pompous. Sometimes I have to laugh to keep from crying. Some of these attorneys are so egotistical. I bent over backwards trying to accommodate him, and he didn't even say thanks. He could have cared less about the record, and he slurred his words which drives me crazy. When I asked him to repeat something that I could not understand, he glared at me with hateful eyes like I was incompetent. Really, Sarah, most people don't realize how stressful being a Court Reporter is at times. Sometimes you feel like screaming right out loud. It gets so tense, especially when the attorneys start talking all over each other. In cases like that, Sarah, I have to get stern with them and tell them that if they want a clean record, then they better speak one at a time. To tell you the truth, some of these attorneys have no idea of how important it is that they speak clearly and only one at a time. Sarah, are you still there? Am I boring you half way to death? I feel like I am rattling on and on."

"No. No. To be honest with you, Allie, I find your occupation to be extremely interesting, more so than most. I would take your place any day just to hear some of those cases, especially the dicey stuff."

I hesitate to say this to Sarah, but I think I will. I want to tell Sarah just a little bit about Rosie without mentioning her name. "Speaking of cases, Sarah, that's why I called you. You know, I can never discuss the Grand Jury proceedings with you, but a strange thing happened to me Tuesday night. I won't even mention the woman's name, but one of the Grand Jury members came up to me after the proceedings. She had tears in her eyes and stated that she wanted to talk to me about something in private. I was, as you can well imagine, startled, but I told her that I was not to talk to any of the Grand Jury members in a private way, never, and that we needed to leave it at that. It has been on my mind ever since. What do you think about that?"

"Hmmm. I don't know what to think. She is more than likely harmless."

"Hope you are right, Sarah. I need to call mother. Talk to you soon. Love you, Sarah."

"I love you too, Allie."

I better call mother right now. "Hi mother."

"How are you Allie"?

"I do not like to be a complainer, mother, but the depositions I have been taking for the last two days have given me high anxiety. I am involved in a vicious divorce case. They are fighting over everything, right down to the silverware.

These cases where people have enormous amounts of money seem to be the worst. I cannot believe how people complicate their lives. The more that I'm exposed to all the crisis that people are involved in, the more I appreciate you and daddy. Thank you for raising us in a loving environment. I mean that with all my heart.

Attending church regularly and having our family prayers together has taught me that no matter what happens in my life, the Lord will help me overcome challenging obstacles that come along.

I also appreciate you and daddy for teaching me how important it is to partake of the sacrament weekly and stay close to the Lord; to lean on him always."

"Allie, you have brought me to tears. You couldn't give your dad and me any better compliment than that. You have given me such joy. I'm all choked up, honey."

"Well, I sincerely mean what I say. I love you and daddy. I better go, mother. I have to get up early in the morning and begin editing. It will be another grueling day."

CHAPTER 9

I don't dare say anything to mother that would upset her regarding Rosie. I guess I shouldn't even have mentioned anything about the case to Sarah, but I didn't say enough to break the Secrecy Oath.

Actually, I feel the need to laugh more at myself. Sometimes I think maybe I am cracking up on certain days. Oh well. I won't be alone at any rate.

First, I would like to watch the ten o'clock news and see if there is anything about the Rita Clark case. Sure enough. They are talking about the fact that Rita Clark, the Channel 8 Special News Reporter, is being investigated by the Grand Jury in Jefferson County. They stated that no one knows much more. They are explaining to the public that the Grand Jury meets as a secret body and everyone will have to wait until after the Grand Jury investigation is over to find out the outcome.

Rita Clark's picture just came across the television screen. I've always been impressed with Rita Clark and her interesting in-debt special series. She is a household name in the Denver area, especially because of some of the controversial stories she has reported on. Now that Rita Clark has become the target of the Grand Jury investigation, she has been put on leave from her job at Channel 8. What a shame. I feel compassion for her.

I woke up bright and early the next morning thinking I should work for a couple of hours. Then I'll go outside and run. Exercise is a top priority for me. So after working two hours, I put on my running shoes and stepped outside.

A spiritual feeling came over me as I ran. The mountains in the distance filled my soul with peace and tranquility. They remind me of Heavenly Father's magnificent creation of the earth. The Rocky Mountain West is so special to me. I have so many fond memories of family get-togethers. I feel nostalgia when I am in the mountains, because I grew up looking out of my living room window at their majestic beauty.

I would love to someday share a cabin nestled up in the aspen trees and evergreens with someone I love. Will I ever get over that intense feeling of love that I felt for Todd Lewis? I don't know if I will ever meet somebody like him again. After all, he was my high school sweetheart. He swept me off my feet from the very first time I met him. Seeing him come up on our front porch in his baseball cap on our first date, I felt like I had been struck by lightning. For me it was love at first sight. He told me later on in our relationship that he felt the same way.

I know he loved me. We laughed a lot together, and he was a good listener. We had so much in common. He felt the same way about our Heavenly Father and our Savior as I do, and he believed with all his heart in the truthfulness of the gospel.

I still will never understand how he could have turned his back on me, not even communicating with me after he returned from his mission to apologize and be honest enough to tell me he had fallen out of love with me. It just does not make sense.

Oh, wow. I need to concentrate on what I'm doing. That vehicle almost hit me. That was a close call. I am shaking. I'm not going to end up in one piece if I don't keep my mind on what I am doing.

When I arrived home, the phone rang. I will bet that is mother calling.

"Hi Allie."

"Mother is that you? It sounds like you have been crying. Why are you crying? I can barely make out what you are trying to say. Please, stop your crying and tell me what has happened."

"Allie, I wanted to touch base with you for a minute to see how you are doing."

"I am just fine." I didn't want to tell mother I almost got hit by a car, and that I'm still in love with Todd. I don't want to worry her to death.

"Allie, wait just a minute. I have a call is coming in. Hang on."

"Sure."

"Allie, sorry to be so long but that was Lydia. She's down in bed and won't be up again until her delivery in July. I have a feeling these next two months are going to be long."

"Mother, I feel so badly that I'm not in a position to help."

"Well, Allie, don't fret so. Your daddy and I are helping with the children, and everybody in Lydia's ward has been so kind and have offered to help in any way they can. You can't believe the food the Relief Society sisters have brought over to her home. I'm so impressed with the generosity and love of the people in Lydia's ward. Why, Allie, they love David and Lydia and the kids so much."

"I know they do, and who wouldn't?"

"You know the place where they serve those great root beer floats?"

"Yes. That sounds so good right now."

"Well, their Home Teachers brought over root beer floats for the entire family the other evening. The children enjoyed the treat so much."

"It is comforting to know that the family is being taken care of so well. Even though I am at a distance from all of you, I can feel the warmth and love."

"Honey, another call is coming in. I'll let you go. Love you so much and take care."

"Love you too, mother." Upon hanging up the phone, I burst into tears. I began to wonder if leaving Utah was the best idea. How I miss my family. I feel so alone right now.

The phone is ringing. "Good morning. Allison speaking."

"Allie, I'm glad you are home."

"Sarah, how are you?"

"I'm great. How are you Allie?"

"A bit depressed. I just talked to mother. She worries so much about Lydia being able to carry the baby to full term."

"Well, Allie, Lydia has so much love surrounding her, she will be just fine. I told her to call me if she needs anything. Your family has been so good to me over the years.

I have great memories of being with you on camping trips, and I'll never forget some of the Family Home Evenings I spent with your family. Because of all of your examples, my testimony has grown. Your family taught me how important it is to stretch and serve the Lord. I love all of you."

"Sarah, that is so sweet of you to say. You are such a special friend to me. We love you too."

"Now for the good news, Allie. Today was an exciting day for me, businesswise. Guess what happened?"

"You met a wonderful man who swept you off your feet."

Sarah laughed. "Well not quite that wonderful, Allie. I sold two of my paintings, one to a Salt Lake City hotel owner and one to the main library here in town."

"Sarah, that is great. You are on your way to being a well-known artist. I can feel it in my bones. I have always known you had it in you. You have been tenacious and continually refused to give up, even when you were harshly criticized. Congratulations. Good for you. It's nice to hear some good news for a change."

"I haven't told you the real good news."

"There is more?"

"Depends on how you look at it. I sold the Rocky Mountain landscape for $24,000 and the Pine View Reservoir painting for $35,000. Well, what do you think of that?"

"Sarah, what can I think? My friend, Sarah, is an artist. Of course, I always knew it, but you had to prove it to yourself."

"Allie, can you get away for a few days? I would love to come over, and we could go up to Estes Park and stay in that wonderful hotel up there. I am looking at some time in July. What do you say?"

"I think it is a great idea, Sarah, but I have so much work to do. In fact, I will be working all weekend on this divorce case that I just took, plus my Grand Jury transcripts have to go out rush after each session. I'm also feeling guilty that I can't be with Lydia to help her out.

Maybe I can fit it in. Meg is great, and I can burn some midnight oil.

"Well, Allie, if you can get your work done, then we could spend Saturday and Sunday in Estes Park, hiking and enjoying the gorgeous Colorado Mountains."

"That sounds fantastic, Sarah. By then, I will need a break more than ever. These long days of working are starting to get to me. It does get to be too much at times."

"Well, Allie, I am going to go to the New York City Art Fair in September. I have several paintings I would like to try and sell and a couple that I'm working on now.

Also, I have been thinking about leaving Utah. After my divorce from A.J., I have felt so lonely. All of our friends are married and having babies. Every shower that I have attended depresses me.

More than anything in the world, we both looked forward to marrying and having a family, and I get pretty frustrated that my life hasn't followed in that direction. I have prayed and prayed that I would find someone to love again, a person who would want to marry me in the temple, someone who would be my eternal mate. I want that more than anything in the world. I'm beginning to feel like a misfit."

"I should not laugh, but please, Sarah, you are anything but a misfit. Please, move to Colorado. You would love it. You could paint to your hearts delight. You could stay with me until you decide to buy yourself a condo or whatever."

"Thank you, Sarah, but I would never ever want to take away your privacy like that. Also, one of the biggest reasons I wouldn't intrude on you is because, as you know, I am a bit messy when it comes to keeping a home tidy.

Besides I appreciate my privacy a lot. I would probably just rent something. What I would really like to do is to rent something in Evergreen, a small cabin, real cozy. I would like to be right in the middle of nature.

I have always loved our cabin up in Ogden Canyon. Over the years I have really enjoyed it. I've been spending a lot of time up there lately painting. The peace and quiet is inviting."

"Sarah, have you talked about your feelings with your mother and dad?" "Yes. Of course, they have been very supportive of me. They do understand."

Changing the subject, can you remember when mother told A.J. that he could go take a flying leap, and that he better well stay away from me? She was like a charging bull. A.J., like I've told you so many times, was impossible to live with. Sometimes you think you know people well when you are dating them, but when they get you wrapped around their little finger, if they don't have good character, proper manners, and some common sense, the relationship can be deadly. They can, without a doubt, fool us."

"Yes, I know exactly what you mean, Sarah."

"Oh, Allie, you were so kind to me during the whole ordeal."

"Well, I heard something that was profound just a few days ago regarding kindness. In essence the man said, "Knowing your own heavy burdens, you should show kindness to others; knowing everyone carries heavy burdens."

"Allie, I like that. I need to write that down."

"Anyway, Sarah, I am going to try my best to get away with you in July. That would be a therapeutic break for both of us. We'll just have to try to make it happen. I would love to escape to the mountains. I know I am repeating myself but you know that I feel so close to God through nature. It does for me what nothing else can.

I need to deliver some pending transcripts to Meg by tomorrow morning. Take care of yourself and, again, congratulations on selling your paintings, Michelangelo. I am proud of you."

"Thanks. Allie, I love you."

"I love you as well." Talking to Sarah seems to have elevated my depressed state of mind. I feel like crying my eyes out. I didn't want Sarah to know it, because she has experienced a few bouts of depression like myself. I definitely experienced a deep depression, especially when Todd disappeared out of my life. Sarah worries about me too much as it is. I just want to cry and cry until the pain finally goes away. I wonder at times if the pain will ever go away. It is impossible to get away from negative memories. At times I feel locked in and not able to get out.

Well, I better get myself together and go to work. This divorce case is something out of a nightmare. It is so tedious. Ralph Monroe's testimony about his precious antique cars and all of the diamonds that the couple own seems unreal to me. There is so much hunger in the world, and then there are those who cannot get enough.

Honestly, I've never met a couple who had so much in the way of material possessions and yet were so miserable. It goes to show you that the gold doesn't always glitter.

I'll send these 100 pages to Meg as soon as I edit them.

I vow that no matter how many hours I work during this busy period of time, I'm still going to get out and exercise every day. It definitely raises my spirits and keeps me in shape.

After exercising, I spent the entire day working. By the time I got to bed it was 9:30 in the evening, and I hate to admit it but I feel exhausted.

CHAPTER 10

The alarm rang at 5:15 the next morning. I have to force myself to get up. It is early, but it is important that I accomplish a lot today. I need to be ready to leave for the Grand Jury session around 6:15 this evening.

I have been so absorbed in working on transcripts today that looking up at the clock, I could not believe it. I muttered: The day is gone. It's time to get ready to go to the Grand Jury session.

I arrived at the courthouse early. Jim McCallister entered the courtroom shortly after I did.

Smiling he asked, "Allison, how are you this evening? Are you ready to go to work?"

I returned a friendly smile and said, "I suppose."

Silently I thought: No use complaining. Yet, already I'm feeling a bit weary. Oh well, what's another five or six hours of work.

Jim spoke with sincerity when he said, "Thanks for getting the transcripts to us so quickly."

The comment made me feel good. "You bet."

I looked up and Rosie appeared and sat down in her assigned seat. I'm not going to make eye contact with her. I've got to act like nothing ever transpired between us.

At seven o'clock sharp the Grand Jury proceedings began. Vincent Pagglione called Morgan Summers to the stand. I administered the oath.

"Ms. Summers, would you please state your full name for the record."

"Morgan Ann Summers."

"And your birth date?"

"September 8, 1967."

"And in what capacity are you involved in this case?"

"I'm the lead investigator."

"Could you relate to the Grand Jurors the steps that were taken to investigate Rita Clark?"

"Well, the first thing we decided to do was find out what Rita Clark had done to get the story on the Pit Bulls. Rita Clark was being filmed regarding a story on the dangers of over-the-counter medications, and a newspaper reporter by the name of Willy had been tracking her every move. Willy was waiting for her to finish with the filming, and when the coast was clear he approached Rita Clark in a friendly manner.

Unbeknownst to Ms. Clark, Willy was wired, and he was hoping to get her in a private location where he could record everything she said. We found out later that Rita Clark had met Willy at different times during her career. He, like Rita Clark, was always out to get a winning story.

Willy asked Rita to go with him for a cup of coffee and have a little chitchat. Willy is a short funny-looking little man. I guess I shouldn't put it that way. He's only five-foot three with sandy hair and small piercing hazel eyes that glare at you. He has a broad nose and a thin mouth. When he smiles, all you can see are a mouthful of yellow-crooked teeth. Apparently Rita had said behind his back that she thought Willy was not someone you could trust.

Anyway, Willy couldn't wait to get Rita Clark alone to see what kind of information he could get out of her. He told me that he felt a sigh of relief when Rita Clark agreed to go with him to the coffee shop around the corner in downtown Denver. Willy said that Rita Clark acted somewhat suspicious at the time, but he thought because he had said some complimentary things about her in the Rocky Mountain News, that that is why she agreed to go with him to the coffee shop.

Willy reiterated that he knew for a fact if Rita Clark found out that he was wired, she would have strangled him on the spot. He mentioned he knew that Rita Clark is a feisty gal, and he certainly, under any circumstances, did not want to tangle with her. Willy explained to me how he was being extraordinarily cautious.

They arrived at the coffee shop and sat down in a booth that offered privacy. When the waitress appeared Willy ordered two cups of coffee and two cheese croissants. He said he then gave Rita some time to talk about herself before asking questions. He began by asking her about all the interesting stories she had been doing on television.

Willy told Rita that the public seemed fascinated by her criminal investigations, and then he praised her for being a very popular lady nowadays. He said he was trying to appear calm, but he told me that inwardly he was shaken. Rita told him that before coming to Denver she had worked at a TV station in Chicago. Willy was waiting for an opportunity to get her on the subject of why she wanted to do a story on Pit Bulls. He also asked her about how she felt about the top ratings that the Pit Bull story ended up getting.

Rita told him, as if he didn't know already, that he, himself, knew what the main objective was. Then she proceeded to say that the Channel 8 producers were ecstatic about the story and went along with it wholeheartedly. She explained to Willy that Channel 8 trusted her judgment on any subject matter she chose to do a story on, particularly because all of her stories were receiving high ratings.

From the investigation, we found out that Channel 8 was more than elated over the top ratings that Rita received. They gave her a pretty good raise from what we understand. Willy's job was to get Rita to tell him about what piqued her interest in the Pit Bull story in the first place. He needed for her to use the exact terminology; that she had staged the whole thing.

He asked Rita Clark about whose Pit Bulls she used to be involved in the story. Rita told him that a friend of hers in Lakewood had three Pit Bulls and he allowed her to film the dogs fighting in his own back yard.

Willy kept complimenting her for how realistic she had made it look. As Willy tells it, because he expressed a great deal of enthusiasm for what Rita had done, she did begin to loosen up. She told him that she had bought some muzzles at the pet store in Lakewood, and one of the videographers, who is a real pet lover, was able to put the Pit Bulls in all kinds of situations, to show the viewers how some of the owners of these dogs torture them to make them vicious, even teaching them to kill their opponent during a fight.

Rita did ask Willy if he could believe how cruel these owners can be to these sweet dogs. Willy informed her that not until he had watched Rita's series was he ever aware that such atrocious things were even going on. Rita began to tell Willy about the fact that raising these Pit Bulls to fight was all in the name of big money.

Then Willy began questioning Rita on what she meant by that. Rita apparently found Willy's lack of knowledge about Pit Bulls somewhat unbelievable. She told him that it was common knowledge among many Pit Bull owners that there are several people in the Denver area that have Pit Bull Rings in their basements, and on the weekends this is what they do for entertainment; actually that this is first-class entertainment for some rich people. She also told Willy that apparently the women get more of a thrill out of watching these dogs fight, get bitten all over, bleed from their wounds, bleed from their nostrils, fight until one drops dead in the ring with blood flowing everywhere.

Blood Sport is common terminology used to describe the sport. Willy told us later that hearing about the bloody details caused him to turn pale, and he felt faint. He told Rita that he couldn't understand why anybody would want to be involved in such wicked actions.

Then Willy became anxious and wanted to get out of there, but he knew that he needed to get the information that he was paid to get as quickly as possible. Rita called Willy a little weasel and asked him why he didn't get it. Willy did not appreciate Rita Clark referring to him as a "little weasel" but did not let on that he was offended. He just replied that maybe he was stupid. Then Rita agreed that maybe he is. She then explained to him again that it was all for big money, big betting going on. Finally Willy lit up and told Rita that he got the picture.

In many ways Rita Clark could be ruthless, and Willy began feeling a bit scared. He felt he had enough information and abruptly looked at his watch and blurted out, "Oh geez, I have an appointment that I forgot about. It was wonderful to see you again, Rita."

Then Rita asked him, "By any chance, Willy, are you wired? Are you?" She moved toward him, wanting to frisk him, but apparently she decided that Willy would not stoop that low. Willy commented in a choked voice, "You have got to be kidding? Got to run, Rita. Nice talking to you."

Before Willy darted out, he threw $20.00 down on the table and stumbled out among the crowd. Rita said on the recorded tape, "You guys are all alike, brainless."

Vincent looked at me and then said, "Okay, we all need to take a break."

Underneath my breath I muttered. Thank you, Vincent. I needed a break in the worst way. I decided to use the bathroom on the lower floor to get away from everyone, especially Rosie.

When I returned from break and sat down ready to proceed, I noticed that the Grand Jurors were stone-faced when they returned to their seats, all except Rosie who seemed to always have that hideous grin on her face, enjoying every minute of the charade.

Ms. Summers returned to the witness stand. She continued to testify for at least three more hours, trying to convince the Grand Jury members that Rita Clark was a first-class criminal, and then they brought in another investigator who was involved in the case, Sandy Williams, who spoke at the rate of 300 words a minute, never catching her breath. Ms. William's testimony droned on and on until one o'clock in the morning, at which time the Grand Jury session adjourned.

I am warped, worn to a frazzle, and by the looks of the Grand Jurors and everybody else, so are they. I'm also very frustrated. Someone always waits for me to walk me to my car. Why has everyone disappeared without a word? I'm not very comfortable being left here alone in the courthouse.

Well, I better move quickly. It is not a very good feeling to be left alone in the courthouse. Strange. For some strange reason, I'm not feeling safe. I'll get my keys ready and make a beeline for my car. I need to make sure that no one is following me.

You know, maybe it is my imagination, but it seems like during the break Vincent, Jim McCallister and Morgan Summers seemed aloof toward me. If I didn't know any better, I would say that they are deliberately avoiding me every chance they get. I'm probably becoming overly sensitive. It could also be the fact that

I've worked so many hours overtime today, and I am more exhausted than usual which lends itself to my mind being cluttered.

Actually, there is no time for pettiness or worrying about what people think. I have to just let go and pray to the Lord for my peace of mind.

I arrived home in good time because there was no traffic on the road. Brewster was at the entrance and waved me on with a big smile. Brewster is a hunk of a guy, weighing around 250 pounds. He is as bald as an Eagle. His dark eyes twinkle. He has a large nose that twitches when he smiles. He is so full of wit. I think he is such a generous man. He loves to tease all of us. On the other hand, he takes his job seriously.

I know for a fact that Brewster gives everybody in the complex a feeling of safety. He can take care of himself in any given situation and the rest of us as well. I have to admit, I'm glad Brewster guards our entrance. He gives me a sense of security, especially because I have definitely felt more uneasy as of late.

I'm certain that nobody could get beyond the stone wall of this complex without Brewster knowing it.

It's early in the morning. I think I'll sleep in. That is the sensible thing to do. First of all, I want to read my Bible for comfort and then I'll say my prayers and hopefully be able to fall asleep.

CHAPTER 11

I stirred when I heard the phone ringing at 10:00 in the morning. What a nightmare I was having. I probably could have slept until noon if the phone had not rung. I am still half asleep.

I picked up the phone. "Good morning."

"Hi Allie."

"Hi Sarah. What are you doing?"

"Well, by Friday there will be a surprise coming for you in the mail, but I am not going to tell you what I am sending you. Hope you like it."

"You are too generous, Sarah. Really and truly, you are. Guess what time I arrived home from the Grand Jury session this morning?"

"Don't ask me to guess."

"I didn't get to bed until two o'clock."

"Allie, you must be exhausted. You never talk about the Grand Jury case you are so heavily involved in. Of course, I understand why. I admit that I can't help being curious. All I can say is, as many hours as you are working, this has got to be some kind of a horrendous crime."

"Whatever."

"Allie, whatever happened to that gal that wanted to be your friend?"

"Oh, that ended up being nothing out of the ordinary. Hey Sarah, what is the surprise?" I realized that I shouldn't mention anything about Rosie again to Sarah or anyone. Rosie's actions that day still alarm me.

"Allie, I bought an airline ticket on American to come and visit you on July 16th. Of course, I realize plans could change, depending on when Lydia has the baby. Is it bad timing for me to come then? Be honest with me. It won't hurt my feelings. Hopefully your workload will lighten up. I understand that right now you are under a lot of pressure."

"No. By that time I will be more than ready for a break. More than likely, even if Lydia delivers at that time, I won't fly home until I can spend at least a week or two with the family. Please, plan to definitely come."

"Allie, I am now in the middle of a painting that I want to finish so that I can exhibit it at the New York City Art Fair. I am pretty excited about the Art Fair, Allie. I wasn't exactly sure if I could pursue this type of a career, but it looks like it's going to happen. I have faith."

"Sarah, ever since I've known you, I have never doubted that you would end up being an artist or do something very creative. Let's face it, your talent is a gift from God. Not everyone can pick up a paint brush and express themselves like you do. Do you want my opinion? The opportunities before you couldn't happen to a more wonderful and spiritual person than yourself."

"I will take that as a compliment coming from you."

"Sarah, I have got to go. I'm on the run. I will be talking to you soon."

"Love you."

"Love you too, Sarah."

I picked up my scriptures and read for 15 minutes. Then I knelt to pray. Negative thoughts are cluttering my mind. For instance, I can't help but think about Todd at times. I'll never understand in a million years why he never spoke a word to me when he returned from his mission. I was distraught.

Mother and daddy were so worried about me. The family worried about me a lot during that time. They wanted to contact Todd themselves to get to the bottom of this unbelievable situation. I begged them not to get involved. I convinced them that if he had fallen out of love with me, what good would it do but only make matters worse. Although I was beside myself trying to figure out why he dropped me so suddenly. It just didn't make sense and still doesn't.

We were deeply in love with each other. I had waited two and a half years for him to return to me and was expecting him to relish the moment when we could embrace each other. Our letters to each other were so tender. We expressed our devotion to each other and wrote about our future plans together. We even talked about going on a mission together in our later years.

Todd destroyed my confidence when he rejected me like that. Thank goodness I have pulled through this trial through the Lord's help and the love of my family and Sarah. Through the teachings of the gospel, I have learned to value my own life in a way that I never realized could be possible.

Now, when I wake up every morning, I thank my Heavenly Father that I have such a wonderful mother and father and sister and brother and the best friends anyone could ever ask for and, of course, good health. I'm appreciative to have a good job that pays me well enough to sustain myself.

The gospel also has taught me to focus on the positive and, of course, the importance of service. Admittedly, after Todd was no longer in my life, it was difficult to think positive. It has been a challenge that I thought I would never have to face, but I now have a stronger testimony through experiencing adversity to understand that this life is a test, and I know that I have to constantly be learning how to cope with whatever comes my way.

When I was lost in the wilderness, I turned to my Heavenly Father and He helped me to get back on the right track. Repeatedly we are being told to endure to the end. I remind myself of that constantly. I am so blessed. There are many more days now that I can say I feel happiness, and I am, more often anyway, at peace.

I need to eat a good breakfast, and then run a few important errands. The Grand Jury session begins at seven o'clock sharp. I've got time to jog and then go over to Meg's house. I can't wait to surprise her.

After I exercised, I went to Meg's home. When I knocked on Meg's door, I did so with anticipation. When Meg answered the door she gave me a big hug.

"Hi Meg." "Hi Allie. You look so cute in your pink jogging outfit."

"Thank you. I have something for you, Meg. Open the envelope."

"You are kidding? $500 Allie. What in the devil is this for?"

"It's for all the hard work you have been doing. I couldn't carry on with all these rush transcripts without you. You have been great."

Meg began to cry and kissed me on the cheek.

"Thank you, Allie. I certainly didn't expect this, but it will come in handy."

"You deserve it more than words can express. You have been caring for your mother for as long as I've known you. You are a saint."

"Oh Allie, that makes me laugh. Saint I am not, but if you think so, I'll enjoy the title. You know, Allie, I used to wonder about you, what you were really like. As difficult as this is to admit, I was always jealous of you when we were at the Academy together. I never knew until I began scoping for you what fine qualities you have, what a wonderful human being you are. You are so sensitive to the needs of others."

"Well, now, don't make me cry. We could just sit here and cry our eyes out and then decide what to do next." I laughed.

"Are you hungry Allie?"

"Well I ate, but I could eat again."

"Come on in the kitchen and have some homemade soup and salad."

"I'll accept that grand invitation, Meg. Your kitchen is so cozy and inviting, and the food looks delicious. Yummy, Meg. You are an excellent cook. I hate to eat and run, but you more than anyone else understands."

"Thank you for your generosity, Allie. Let me hug you again before you go."

I drove home and worked on transcripts and then quickly got ready so I would be at the courthouse earlier than usual.

As I drove to the courthouse, I couldn't help thinking about Rita Clark and the fact that she will be testifying tonight. This evening ought to be interesting. I wonder if she looks the same as she does on television. Her personality is delightful and she seems so nice. Admittedly, she has a real unique way of telling a story. From what I have heard from the witness stand so far, there doesn't seem to be much of a chance that Rita Clark will be indicted for staging a story. What do I know?

Well, maybe the D.A.'s are so desperate for cases to come before the Grand Jury to keep them busy, that when they got wind of this horrific crime that Rita Clark has committed, they decided that it warranted a Grand Jury investigation, or could there be another point to this? Maybe she has done something in the past that infuriated them, and they are retaliating against her.

I actually think Vincent Pagglione is getting too big for his own britches. One thing for certain, he has his fingers wrapped around all the Judges in Jefferson County. I cannot help but feel amused. I will give him credit for one thing. He is a born politician, not to mention his impressive social connections.

Well, I'm here in the courtroom in plenty of time and have all my equipment setup and ready to go. I wonder where everyone is. It is unusual for Vincent and Jim McCallister not to be present. They are always here a few minutes after I arrive. It's seven o'clock sharp. Here they come, Pagglione, McCallister, and Morgan Summers. Pagglione swaggers as he walks.

How lucky am I? They are nodding at me in a very cold manner. What did I do to deserve such hostile treatment? They are acting more distant from me as this case continues forward. I do not understand their unfriendliness. The Grand Jurors are filing in from the jury room. These Grand Jury sessions are becoming stranger by the minute. I never know what to expect anymore.

Vincent is gesturing to me that he is ready to go on the record. He begins with opening remarks. He is now addressing the Grand Jury members in a more serious tone of voice.

"Members of the Grand Jury. Rita Clark will be appearing this evening along with her attorney, Sinclair Bennett. I can feel trouble brewing. Already there is a nervous tension in the courtroom and my stomach feels sick. This investigation is a travesty as far as I'm concerned. Maybe I'm missing something, but this case is a waste of the tax payer's money.

Rita Clark and her attorney, Sinclair Bennett are entering the courtroom. I cannot help but admire her. She looks smart in her navy blue suit. She is an attractive woman. I like the style of hair. It's short and sassy. She has beautiful blue eyes. Her smile reveals perfect white teeth, and her makeup is applied tastefully.

She does seem to have a lot of confidence. Rita Clark's attorney is handsome. He is around six-foot one with curly brown hair and big brown eyes. Both Rita Clark and Sinclair Bennett are being asked to raise their right hand. Vincent Pagglione is putting them under oath. He then begins to speak:

> "Members of the Jury, I would like to introduce you to Rita Clark and Sinclair Bennett. I want to explain to you again that Rita Clark, under the Rules, can have her attorney, Sinclair Bennett, present during her testimony. The Grand Jury Rules state that her attorney can be present with her, but he is not allowed to say a word. He is not allowed to coach Ms. Clark as to how she should answer any of the questions."

Vincent Pagglione begins the questioning of Rita Clark.

"Ms. Clark, would you please state your full name for the record."

"Rita Samantha Clark."

"And your date of birth."

"April 16, 1960."

"And your educational background. Just briefly, please.

"I attended Wellsley and received my degree in journalism, and when I moved out to Colorado I began taking classes in broadcasting at Denver University. "

"Are you married?"

"Yes, I am."

"What is your husband's occupation?"

"He has his own computer business, Clark and Clark Associates."

"Do you have any children?"

"No, Mr. Pagglione. At this time, realizing my clock is ticking, I don't know if that will be in the future or not. My career has been my main focus, and I have put all my energy in my profession. It is something I enjoy very much, something that I have wanted to do since I was a little girl, and when the opportunity came up to be a Television Reporter for Channel 8, I was thrilled."

"Tell us how you came about wanting to do a story on Pit Bulls."

"Well, we were at a party and a man that was present was talking about a friend he had who had a Pit Bull Ring on his premises, and this man and his wife, mind you, had been present several times enjoying watching these Pit Bulls fight until one dies a horrific death.

Needless to say I was shocked. I didn't know this type of devilish activity was happening so often in the Denver area or, as I found out later, nationwide. I'm a lover of dogs, and I was very upset that such a gruesome activity was ongoing in our community. Worse still, the people attending these dog fights would bet on who would win, and then I began to realize, after the man kept telling us about the details, that a great deal of money is involved. So I decided that I wanted to do a story and expose these monsters that are training these dogs to be killers."

"What did you do next"?

"I bought some muzzles and used the Channel 8 photographers to do the videoing of the Pit Bulls. I made arrangements to have the filming done in the back yard of a friend's home in Lakewood. There was a great deal of preparation beforehand as we had to acquire a lot of information in order that we could convey to the public the brutality that was taking place; mainly that these Pit Bulls viciously are being trained to kill.

To me, it is criminal to mistreat any dog, especially to train them to fight to kill. It is inhumane, to say the least, and it should not be tolerated."

"Thank you, Ms. Clark. Jim McCallister has some questions for you."

Jim McCallister had Rita Clark on the witness stand for two and a half hours, and then he asked the Grand Jurors if they had any questions. The Grand Jurors asked Rita Clark several questions. The Grand Jury Rules allow them to ask anything they want to, ridiculous or not.

Rosie, always wanting to be center stage, asks a lot of questions. Her questions are definitely not on point at all. They don't even relate to the investigation. I'm beginning to wonder if she actually understands what's going on.

After a break, the testimony of Rita Clark continued until around 12:15 a.m. in the morning, at which time Rita Clark and her attorney were excused.

With a sigh of relief, I mumbled: Thank goodness we are finished.

After Rita Clark and Sinclair Bennett left the courtroom, Pagglione began talking to the Grand Jury members regarding what had transpired that evening during the questioning and answering process.

I am still on the record as far as I am concerned. What happened next threw me for a loop. It was Pagglione who looked straight at me and said, "This will be off the record."

Off the record? I mumbled to myself. What is he saying? Something is going on here that is disturbing. I never have gone off the record in a Grand Jury session before. I had worked with Chief District Attorney Adams for four and a half years, before Vincent came on the scene, and Adams was adamant about making sure that everything that was being said in the Grand Jury proceedings was on the record. That meant at all times. I understood that from the beginning when I was sworn in to be the Grand Jury Reporter for Jefferson County. In fact, I know the Grand Jury Rules; that all the colloquy, the conversations between the Grand Jurors and the District Attorneys, or the investigators, should be on the record.

What is Pagglione up to? I am flabbergasted by his actions. I feel numb. I don't want anything to do with this horrific situation I find myself in. Ooooh! He's saying that Rita Clark's attorney, Sinclair Bennett is a bumbling idiot. Now he's saying that Rita Clark was evasive and distorted the facts in her testimony this evening. He's painting a picture to the Grand Jurors of the seriousness of the crimes Rita Clark has committed. He is criticizing her, saying she is overly-confident and that she thinks she hasn't done anything wrong.

I feel very uneasy, not to mention that this is scary. Pagglione is trying to manipulate these Grand Jurors. If you ask me, he's making a mountain out of a molehill and creating in the Grand Jurors' minds that what Rita Clark did is the crime of the century. Well, in my opinion, everything that is coming out of his big mouth is a rotten lie. Here I sit, realizing I am not supposed to be off the record, and I can't help but feel terrified. I hope I don't throw up right here and now.

Pagglione is putting me in a position of being part of some criminal conspiracy. If they think that what Rita Clark has done is in the category of some kind of a terrible crime, what they are doing here, as far as going off the record, is a much more serious crime. It places me in a very fearful situation that I do not want anything to do with.

The D.A.'s and investigators are attacking Rita Clark's character and saying absolutely hideous things about Sinclair Bennett. Goodness, these words should not be uttered about any person on or off the record.

I know my face is flushed. Jim McCallister is pointing at me. Now what? McCallister stated, "That wasn't on the record, was it, Allison?"

I nodded. My whole body is shaking. I don't even know if I nodded my head from side to side or up and down. I'm in such a state of high anxiety. Now Pagglione is speaking.

"Members of the Grand Jury: I want to remind you of the Secrecy Oath you took at the beginning of your service. I know you realize the importance of abiding by that oath. Again, you need to take this case very seriously. You should not, under any circumstances, ever discuss anything to anyone regarding what goes on during these Grand Jury proceedings. With that instruction, you are excused, and I want to thank you for your service."

I stood up as the Grand Jurors filed out. My legs are shaking. I then nervously began packing my equipment. Vincent approached me and said in a very stern and abrupt manner: "Hey, Allison. Don't put that blurb in the transcript regarding that we were off the record. Understand?"

I know my face is showing my frustration. I can't even think straight. Should I go along with this dastardly deed or what? All my life my mother and father have taught me to be honest. One thing for sure, these high-powered District Attorneys can be beyond frightening. I know what has happened to a few people who have crossed them.

My voice was shaking when I answered. "Sure, Vincent. I understand."

"Good girl. And Allison, don't you forget the oath that you took when you were sworn in. It's very serious if any leaks come out of these Grand Jury proceedings regarding any cases that we are investigating. We work together as a team, right?"

By this time I am speechless. "Uh-huh."

My mind is filled with remorse. Of course, I don't want to be a part of Vincent's team. I am terrified. Do not involve me in this devilish act, Vincent.

The team swaggered out of the courtroom leaving me alone again without an escort to take me to my car. I do not trust any of them anyway. To make matters worse, there is no guard on duty at the courthouse. I can't believe this is happening. What are they up to, and why are they becoming so aloof towards me? Why? As if I didn't know. They are using dangerous tactics with these Grand Jurors, and the Grand Jurors are like putty in their hands, completely unaware of what is going on. They are being used as pawns so that the D.A.'s can be certain that Rita Clark will be indicted. They are going all out to viciously attack Rita Clark, deliberately trying to ruin her reputation and to make sure that she pays a heavy price.

How puzzling this is for me as well as extremely dangerous. I may never really know the answer as to why. I'm so nervous. What am I going to do? Fearful as I am, I have to use good judgment by playing my cards right or I will be their next target because of what I know at this point.

I can't go and talk to Chief Judge Zacharelli. Vincent and Zacharelli are very close-knit. Unfortunate as it is, I am going to have to grin and bear it, and pray to Heavenly Father that it doesn't continue on until next year. This is some kind of a personal vendetta to go after Rita Clark for something she probably did in the past other than this absurd Pit Bull story. It has got to be.

I have my car keys in my hand. I am trying to be cautious. I will hurry and open the trunk and put my equipment inside. It is dark out and spooky. I looked carefully over my shoulder more than once before I put my key in the ignition. I guess it is safe.

When I arrived home, I was a nervous wreck. I double-locked my front door once I got inside, and then proceeded to double-lock all of the other doors. I am beginning to question my own sanity, and I feel so alone in this unbelievable situation.

Should I tell mother or Sarah? No. I am not to discuss anything of what happens in Grand Jury proceedings. I am bound by the Grand Jury Secrecy Oath.

I can't help but wonder what Rita Clark did to make these guys go after her like sharks. Maybe she belittled them on Channel 8 News. I swear, I am driving myself crazy with asking so many questions that are on my mind. I obviously have no answers, no concrete answers. For certain Rita Clark has made them furious in some way, furious enough for them to go after her with a vengeance.

I'm now afraid to go to the next Grand Jury session. I think I will close these drapes carefully. Then I feel a need to kneel down and ask my Heavenly Father for protection. Pagglione looked at me in the courtroom in such an odd way as if to say, if you know what's good for you, you'll keep your mouth shut.

I know one thing for certain. Vincent Pagglione hates me. I will kneel down and pray to my Heavenly Father with all my heart. Then I'll read my scriptures if I can concentrate. They always give me such comfort. I don't think I am going to be able to sleep. After I fervently prayed, I opened my Bible and turned to Proverbs.

CHAPTER 12

Finally I was able to doze off at 4:00 in the morning. I slept for a few hours and then got up, ate and began working on the Rita Clark transcript. I have been thinking about what angers me more than anything is that these District Attorneys are in a position to run their own Grand Jury show with no one looking over their shoulders, and they know it.

I feel trapped because I am in a dangerous situation, and all I can do is hold on tight and try to weather the storm. I've figured out at this point that Rosie, with her grandiose questions, was not selected at random to serve as a Grand Juror.

My phone is ringing.

"Hi Allie."

"Hi Meg. What do you need, love?"

"Just a few questions. Allie, you sound exhausted. I know you are not getting enough rest."

"I agree with what you are saying, Meg, but we have to do our job, right?" "Right. Hey, Allie, the questions can wait. I'll write them down so I won't forget to ask you."

"Okay. Meg, I want to pay you rush rates."

"Allie, you are a doll, you know it. Most Court Reporters don't care anymore about what they pay you. In fact, some of the other Court Reporters I do work for, they don't care if you work overtime or not. They won't pay you anymore on a rush transcript. They don't offer me a penny more than their standard rate, even though I know they are getting paid plenty for rush jobs."

"That is unconscionable. Meg, speak up."

"I know. Well, sometimes I feel so insecure about my finances that I'm afraid if I tell some of the Court Reporters I work for the truth they will look for someone else. In all honesty, I would prefer to work for you exclusively, but right now I don't have a choice."

"Meg, let's face it, we're all a bunch of dingbats. That's a prerequisite for this type of job."

"I don't put you in their category of being a dingbat, Allie."

"You're sweet but, honey, on any given day you could put me in that category.

On a serious note, Meg, just a reminder. Remember that no leaks of any kind should ever come out of the Grand Jury proceedings. So be careful. I, myself, am feeling more paranoid than usual lately. I know you understand the Grand Jury Secrecy Rules and take the Grand Jury Oath as seriously as I do, but I haven't said much to you regarding this subject as of late. Just to reiterate, I know you are aware that you should never speak to anybody about a case that is in progress or any of the previous cases that we have worked on together."

"Allie, I would be terrified to ever talk about any of the cases to anyone. I understand my responsibility, and I do take it very seriously."

"I know you do, but I just thought I would mention it again, just as a reminder. Talk to you soon, and if you have any questions, please don't hesitate to call me. I want to expedite these transcripts as smoothly as possible. We have to please the General."

"I hear you. Talk to you later, Allie."

"Okay. I'll call you on Saturday to see how things are progressing."

"Thanks, Allie. Get some rest."

"Thank you, Meg. Have a great day."

Let's see, I said to myself: I have to work long hours, but I refuse to work on the Lord's Day. Partaking of the sacrament on Sunday's is an important spiritual experience for me. It is the least I can do in remembrance of how much the Savior has sacrificed for me.

I realize that I can't take all of the depositions that I have booked. Ginger will always help me out. I know I can count on her.

Sometimes this feeling of fear that I have is something I can't seem to shake, especially when I think about the predicament I am in. I'm starting to realize that I'm being used as a pawn myself, and the only thing that I can do for solace is to lean on the Lord.

I hear the phone ringing.

"Hey Allie, this is Brewster. You have a large package that was just delivered."

"Thanks Brewster. I'll be right over to pick it up."

"Hey, beautiful, I'll bring it over to you. It is too heavy for you to carry."

"Thank you, Brewster, for being so thoughtful."

"No problem. I'll set it on your porch and be gone in a flash."

When I opened my front door, there was a large package for me. I am so excited to open this up. What in the world could it be? So this is the surprise that Sarah was talking about on the phone. I opened the box as quickly as I could. It's her beautiful painting of Longs Peak. She knows how much I love this area. It is one of my favorite mountainous areas near Estes Park.

I'm in complete amazement. I want to cry thinking about the generosity of Sarah. I feel loved. Sarah's landscape paintings are, without a doubt, her forte. She is so talented. She painted this on a day when the mountains were snowcapped. Oh, the evergreen trees are rising majestically at the base of the mountain, and the aspen trees are in the foreground. Bless her. She knows aspen trees are my favorite. I am absolutely thrilled. I've got to call her."

"Sarah, pick up the phone."

"Hi Sarah." I am crying at this point.

"Sarah, thank you from the bottom of my heart. I received the painting a few minutes ago. You can't imagine how much this means to me. You made my day. Your thoughtfulness is beyond belief. You must have read my mind, because down deep

I was wanting one of your paintings, but I wasn't sure I could afford your prices." We both laughed simultaneously.

"I have already designated a spot to hang it, over the fireplace, and I will treasure it forever. I am crying out of sheer joy."

Sarah paused and with a huge smile on her face said, "Allie, don't cry. Silly. I loved painting it for you, and I thoroughly enjoyed being at Longs Peak to do the sketch. I felt so serene during the time we were there. Hey, we need to do that hike again if we end up going to Estes Park."

"That would be wonderful. Sarah, I'm going to work long hours until I go to the Grand Jury session on Tuesday night. I've made it a point not to work on Sunday no matter what.

I look forward to the trip to Estes Park. It will be a much needed break for both of us. The thought of being in the Colorado Rockies elevates my mood. Love you. Thanks again."

"I am choked up with emotion to where I can hardly speak. Allie, you are and always have been a wonderful example to me. If you can't talk to me on Saturday, I understand, but then call me on Sunday, okay?"

"Okay. Thank you again, Sarah. Take care."

Tuesday rolled around too soon for me. It is time for another Grand Jury session.

CHAPTER 13

I always used to look forward to going to the Grand Jury sessions, and now I'm dreading it. I know, without a doubt, I'm going to have to face the facts about this situation. I also know that without the Savior in my life, I couldn't make it through this challenging time.

I arrived at the courthouse with a knot in the pit of my stomach.

Vincent Pagglione, Jim McCallister and Morgan Summers briskly walked in the courtroom precisely at seven o'clock sharp. I looked at them in disgust. My oh my, they certainly have a pompous air about them. Who do they think they are fooling? Unfortunately, they are fooling these Grand Jurors to the max and more unfortunate than that is they are getting away with it.

Vincent is nodding at me to go on the record. "Okay, Members of the Grand Jury, we are on the record." He is forcing a smile as he looked at me. I feel flushed and terribly uncomfortable already.

"We will call John Barker to the stand." Vincent blurted this out in his overconfident manner. John Barker, together with Sam Lucas, are the videographers that did the filming of the Pit Bulls at the Lakewood location, showing in detail the various ways the dogs were tortured; the malicious techniques the trainers use to teach the dogs to be killers.

John Barker is about six feet tall, a burly man. His hair is thinning and the color is salt and pepper. He has large blue eyes, a prominent nose and a strong jaw. His ruddy complexion tells the story of a man who has spent many an hour in the bar; that he has had his knocks in life. You can tell that he is a man who is not easily intimidated.

Mr. Barker was administered the oath by Vincent, and the testimony began with Vincent asking the questions.

"State your name."

"John Barker."

Vincent questioned him for almost an hour regarding his educational background and experience as a photographer and videographer.

I could tell at this point that it wouldn't take much more for John Barker to become angry. I can see that he is on edge. John Barker is a true veteran in his field. He isn't about to take any nonsense from Vincent.

His answers are direct, only giving the details necessary, and he looks directly at the jurors. John Barker is well aware that he could be charged with a felony or two himself for being a part of all this.

Vincent appears to be unaware of the potential of his witness becoming angry. He is too caught up in himself.

I am feeling uneasy because of Vincent's rudeness towards Barker. I am so annoyed. Vincent is so stupid. He is harassing Barker. Anyone with any common sense would handle him more tactfully.

I can't believe John Barker did not bring in an attorney with him. I admire his guts. He doesn't seem to be afraid of too much of anything like most people would be in his situation. John Barker's face is furious because Vincent is asking him about his experience in Viet Nam and if it is a fact that he was the lead photographer in the war, taking pictures of some horrendous atrocities.

I am beginning to feel a tinge of fear. I'm astonished. The questions Vincent is firing at Mr. Barker are infuriating him. I wouldn't doubt it one bit if Barker jumps out of the witness chair and pops Vincent a good one alongside of the head. He deserves it. I can tell from Barker's demeanor that he is doing his very best to control himself.

Geez, I'm wondering if this badgering will ever end. I feel absolutely miserable, not to mention that the Grand Jurors, from the expressions on their faces, have had just about enough.

Give it up, Vincent. One day you will get your dues. I know when it really gets bad, because I have a tendency to grit my teeth.

The Grand Jury session ended at 1:15 a.m. John Barker was asked to return on the following Thursday. I am worn out. Look at the jurors. They are totally exhausted. The mood has been extremely tense for all of us. Even Rosie, thank The Lord, gave up on asking so many ridiculous questions.

Thank goodness Vincent did not go off the record tonight. It saved me from going into orbit. I don't think Vincent realizes how wicked his approach can be. He is so self-absorbed.

Anyway, I am so relieved to pack up and leave as quickly as possible. I am continually looking over my shoulder when I leave the courthouse. It has become a habit. You never know who might be lurking. Even if someone is watching me or deliberately wanting to harm me, it is just as well that I don't know, because I would feel extreme fear.

In fact, Allison is being followed by a man driving a Maserati. The man is rugged looking. He is 43 years of age and has a thick head of wavy black hair and deep colored eyes. He is wearing dark sunglasses. His face reveals a deep scar on his left side below the eyebrow. His name is Dino. He is wearing black leather pants and a black leather jacket with a multicolored symbol painted on one sleeve. He is built like a football player. His appearance is frightening. He is someone you would want to avoid if you happened to meet him on the street. You would instantly feel the urge to get out of the way of such an individual. Dino's radio blared with the sound of Hard Rock music. A cigarette is dangling out of his mouth.

CHAPTER 14

I arrived home, thinking that I better lock up all the entrances to my condo. All of a sudden I felt a strong desire to kneel down and pray. A sweet spirit began to enter my body. After I said my prayers, I read from the Old Testament. I get a lot of inspiration by reading Isaiah. He is one of the greatest prophets to ever live, as well as being a poet. After reading Isaiah, I feel more relaxed. I took a deep breath. I feel such love and gratitude in my heart for all my blessings.

After a good eight hours of sleep, I awoke to the sweet sound of birds singing. I stretched and thought to myself: This morning I feel more peaceful. I know I'm being protected. I looked in the bathroom mirror and thought I looked more rested.

The phone is ringing.

"Allie."

"Hi mother. How is everything?" "Good, honey. Lydia is obeying the doctor's rules and enjoying the children's company. They cuddle up with her and talk and laugh. The sisters in her ward have bent over backwards to help her. There is always a hot meal being delivered daily by someone with love. It's humbling. Oddly enough, sometimes when you are forced to slow down, other treasured moments happen in your life. You begin to realize how important family and friends are. One thing for certain, Allie, through adversity, our priorities certainly change."

"Truer words were never spoken, mother."

"Your daddy and I are trying to do a temple session every week. Oh, Allie, there is such a beautiful spirit in the temple. When I enter the temple, I feel as if I've left this world behind. It is more spiritual than anything I've ever experienced in my life. Your daddy and I, when we leave the temple, we have both commented to each other how we feel renewed, blessed beyond measure."

"Oh, mother."

"What honey?"

"I sometimes wonder if I will ever fall in love again. I want what you and daddy have. I want someone just like my daddy to take me to the temple to be married for time and all eternity. That has always been my dream. Mother, don't cry."

"Sweetheart, if you will be patient it will happen. I know how much you adored Todd. We adored him too. We thought he was the perfect match for you. We still talk about how bizarre everything turned out. I know love when I see it, and Todd was head over heels for you."

"Well, mother, I thought so too, but apparently we all were blinded by some unknown factors. Through prayer and having so many blessings and being able to express my feelings with the Bishop, I'm healing, and I know you and daddy are too, as well as Mitch and Lydia. All of you couldn't have been more loving and compassionate to me.

Little by little I'm moving on, trying to live the commandments of our Savior and being grateful every day for all that I've been given spiritually.

I want to say something, mother. You have been the most wonderful example in my life. I've watched you give and give and give throughout your life. And do you know what? I want to be just like you when I grow up."

"Oh Allie, I'm laughing and crying at the same time. You have touched me deeply. Your daddy and I are so thrilled to have two daughters and a son that, through trials and tribulations, have given us the inner strength to carry on.

Allie, honey, I have to go. I'll fill your daddy in on everything. He gives you his love and can't wait to see you. Hopefully, as soon as you are out from under your workload, you can spend some time with us."

"I can't wait, mother."

"Love you, more than words can express, honey."

"Love you too, mother. Give hugs and kisses to daddy, Lydia and David and the kids, and, of course, my adorable brother, Mitch."

"I will Allie."

I feel depressed after talking to mother. I miss her and the family so much. Mother always tries to lift my spirits, and I don't want my thoughts to go to the negative. Well, how can I be depressed with such a loving family? I want to be careful what I say to mother and daddy. They would be worried out of their minds if they knew what was going on. I know with God's help and if I stay attuned to the sweet spirit of our Savior, I will be protected from any harm.

I better get to work. I need to remind myself to eat nutritiously and exercise daily in order to stay mentally alert. I'm not getting enough sleep. Being deprived of sleep is making me have mood swings, more than I ever have in my life. I am concerned about those dark circles under my eyes.

The Grand Jury session met again on Thursday, and John Barker was asked to resume his seat on the witness stand. Vincent reminded him that he had previously been placed under oath. John Barker and Sam Lucas both testified that evening, and it was more or less the same testimony that, yes, they had filmed the Pit Bulls showing how the trainers tortured these dogs to be killers. The testimony droned on until 2:30 in the morning.

They finished the testimonies of both videographers, John Barker and Sam Lucas. I muttered to myself: I might as well look at this case as advantageous to me monetarily. Actually, if I'm totally honest, I have to admit that no amount of money is worth this agony. More than likely, the amount of hours I have been working could end up putting me in the grave before my time.

Vincent is telling the Jurors that Rita Clark would be returning to testify on the following Tuesday, June 8th. I groaned. I'm beginning to hyperventilate at the mention of Rita Clark's name. Vincent reminded the Grand Jurors of the Grand Jury Secrecy Oath, and then they were dismissed. Oh, no, Vincent is approaching me. Now what? He is scowling.

"Allison," Pagglione said in a stern voice. "Got a minute?"

"Sure."

"This is about something I thought you ought to know, okay?"

"Yeah." My head is pounding.

"Well, it looks like this case may wind up quicker than we thought. We may be looking at the end of October."

"That's great. I was planning a family get-together around that time. You made my day."

"Well, okay. Allison, I'm rushed as usual. See you next session."

"Thank you for the good news." He didn't, as usual, offer to wait for me so I wouldn't have to leave the courthouse on my own. I need to be cautious, more than I'm accustomed to being. It's close to 3:00 a.m. I never have felt this uneasy in my life. I don't know if I'm becoming unduly paranoid, but I feel like someone is following me.

When I arrived at my condo I muttered: Home at last. Kneeling by my bedside that early morning, I asked Heavenly Father to help me to stay attuned to the spirit of Christ for guidance and comfort.

Upon waking at 10:30 the next morning, before I said my prayers, I turned to some passages of scripture from the Doctrine and Covenants. I don't feel like eating. My appetite is beginning to diminish. I don't feel as confident about myself either. Everything seems to be more difficult for me. These long sessions in Grand Jury are getting me down. It won't be that much longer, and then I can get my life back to normal. Prayer does help immensely regarding the anxiety that is building within me.

The weekend went by uneventful, except I was uplifted from what was said during sacrament meeting about the fact that adversity can give us more strength than we realize; that adversity builds character; that this earth is just a testing ground with many challenges along the way, but what we have to look forward to is the glorious gift of eternity.

CHAPTER 15

I cannot believe that it is time for another session of Grand Jury. It is Tuesday already. I'm beginning to feel that pang of nervousness, and I know for a fact it is worsening because Rita Clark is coming in for further testimony.

I want to call Sarah before I leave. It's extremely important that I'm careful not to alarm her.

"Sarah, hi. I wanted to talk to you before I leave for Grand Jury. I am a bit under the weather. This particular case that we have been working on in the Grand Jury has just about driven me crazy. It doesn't seem to come to an end. It seems to go on and on.

I'm praying and depending on Heavenly Father to help me survive. I am probably being a bit overly dramatic. Sorry for complaining. On the upside, I am looking forward to seeing you in July. We most definitely will need a break at that point."

"Allie, you don't even sound like yourself. I think it would be wise for you to get enough rest, please, and slow down."

"I will be able to do that sooner than I thought. The case may possibly be completed near the end of October. So, thank goodness, I will be freed up to get back to living normal again."

"Listen, Allie, any time you need me, please let me know. If you want my support, I can fly over to help you. You know, if you say the word, I will be there immediately.

Maybe I can cheer you up by telling you that I am getting ready for the big Art Fair in New York City. It's exciting. It will be quite an event, Allie, with artists coming from all over the world to display their art. It's the only thing that keeps me going right now."

"Well, you are headed in the right direction, Sarah. You definitely have what it takes, and don't you forget that. By the way, your painting is hanging above the fireplace, and it is so lovely. The natural wood frame just blends wonderfully well with my decor. Thank you again for being so thoughtful. I don't know what I would have done without your friendship early on in my life. You have been a wonderful friend and stuck by me through all the mourning I did over Todd.

Of late, trust is becoming such an issue with me. Sometimes I feel that I will never be able to trust again. That's a terrible way to be, don't you think?"

"Well, that's to be expected, Allie, after what you have been through, but maybe that will change in time. Just give it time, and don't expect too much out of life. Try to take it as it comes and good things will come your way. You just wait and see."

"Thanks, Sarah. I will do that. I just wanted to check on you to make sure that you are alright. I am going to a Grand Jury session this evening, and just between you and me I am beginning to dread the whole situation. I wish I could talk to you and my family about what's going on, but, you know, that is impossible."

"I have to admit, Allie, I am more than curious. Your type of work fascinates me. To think that you get to hear things that most people never in their lifetime get to hear. I am nosey enough to think that I would have enjoyed a job like yours."

I laughed. "Yes. I am sure in that regard you would have. Well, yes, it is fascinating to watch people and listen to them tell the stories of their lives, but sometimes, truly, it can get to you emotionally.

The only thing is, you have to, at times, try to remove yourself from the situation, and in some cases that is easier said than done. I have cried, laughed, wanted to scream out loud in some of these cases, and actually, on occasion, I have had a strong desire to punch some attorneys in the face for their extremely bad behavior toward certain witnesses, or because they talk so fast that I have felt like throwing my hands up in the air. I have had to be stern at times with certain attorneys and told them that if they want a clean record they better not talk over each other and they needed to enunciate their words.

You have to be in control of the situation. It is not always easy. I do have compassion for people, and when I see a person being treated unfairly, it is more than I can handle sometimes."

"Yes, I am sure that would be true of you. Well, I admire you for being able to take down all of those words at a high rate of speed. I still can't figure out how you do it. Anyway, it certainly does amaze me."

"Me too. Believe you me, I sweat blood sometimes, Sarah. It's just that I don't say much about it. At times you will get these lawyers who don't understand one word about how to make a clean record. They talk all over each other and interrupt each other without a thought about how the record will look afterwards. Then at times people talk with heavy accents that will make you feel like you'd like to tear your hair out. When that happens, I immediately ask for an interpreter knowing full well that if I don't hear what is being said nobody else does either. It's my responsibility to speak up.

Anyway, I hate to bore you with this stuff any longer. Take care, and I will be talking to you soon."

"It doesn't bore me in the least. I have to admit that I am dying of curiosity of what has caused you to be so agitated. I don't remember a case that you have taken that seems so intriguing or that has put you so much on edge. Hey, I'll let you go. Talk to you later. Call me, no matter what time of day or night, if you need to talk. I mean it. Love you, Allie."

"Love you too, Sarah."

CHAPTER 16

I arrived at the courthouse before anybody else. I set up my equipment and hurried to the bathroom. I feel confused. I'm not in the best of shape emotionally. My stomach feels like it is tied in knots. Gee, I better get back to the courtroom. I'm blurry-eyed for some unknown reason. The Grand Jury members are beginning to look unfamiliar to me, like a bunch of people from another planet.

The Grand Jury session began promptly at 7:00. Vincent Pagglione made a few brief comments, and then called Rita Clark to the witness stand. She was reminded of the Oath of Secrecy that she had taken previously.

"Ms. Clark, when you testified last time, did you say that you have two dogs yourself?"

"Yes. I have two Alaskan Malamutes, and to be honest with you, since this case began, I have been so worried about them that I have kept them inside for most of the time unless I am out walking with them. I worry about their safety."

Wow, I thought: I can't believe the change in Rita Clark. She doesn't act like the confident and bubbly person she was when she testified the first time. In fact, she is much more serious. She looks completely worn out. Come to think about it, Sinclair Bennett, her attorney, is much more subdued than he was previously. I'll bet that both of them are starting to get worried about the outcome of this case.

Vincent Pagglione continued:

"What do you mean when you say you are worried about your dogs' safety?"

Oh, I feel agitated. Vincent is up to his tactics again, setting a trap for her. He is deliberately attempting to put her on the defensive and make her a nervous wreck emotionally.

"Well, Mr. Pagglione, I have reason to be worried. Several times over the last few months a dark blue truck has gone by my home. Very suspicious, I thought. To tell you the truth, it terrifies me to think of anything happening to my dogs. They are my life. I love them so much, more than you can imagine."

Vincent continues to ask so many repetitive questions. He already asked some of these questions the first time Rita Clark was on the witness stand. He should be ashamed. He's badgering her to death. At this point, I feel sorry for her.

I'm beginning to feel sorry for myself as well. All I keep thinking about is that Rita Clark must have done something horrendous to them at one time or another that infuriated them, and they are retaliating against her. That's an assumption on my part. All I can do is try to stay calm knowing this nightmare will not last forever. Thank goodness, we are going to take a brief recess.

I wonder why Rita Clark and Sinclair Bennett are rushing out of the courtroom.

Before the Grand Jury members and I were excused to take a break, lo and behold, Vincent Pagglione began to speak to the Grand Jurors, and as he did so he looked at me with an evil eye and said, "This will be off the record."

Now, I feel unhinged. Here we go again. Oh my gosh, they are making fun of Sinclair Bennett, and they are mocking Rita Clark. They are trying with all their might to convince the Grand Jurors into thinking that Rita Clark has been lying from day one when she testified before them and that she is nothing but a common criminal.

I am having difficulty focusing. My hands are shaking. My stomach feels upset. I've got to settle down. What can I do? I can't go to the Judges. All of these judges and D.A.'s stick together like glue. I feel absolutely at their mercy. This case is completely out of control. Vincent Pagglione has involved me. How dare he? This is some sort of a conspiracy to make certain Rita Clark is indicted as well as the videographers.

You do not ever go off the record, Vincent Pagglione. I am doing just that. I am implicated. I will bet that Morgan Summers is looking straight at my fingers right now to make sure that I am not writing. I'm sitting here feeling scared to death and too afraid to speak up. Oh, Lord, please help me. I am so deeply involved in this case. I don't even know how to extricate myself.

Mother and daddy wouldn't believe it. All my life I've been taught how important it is to be honest. They have been carrying on for at least fifteen minutes. How disrespectful to criticize and mock Rita Clark and Sinclair Bennett. Here they come. Rita Clark and Sinclair Bennett are returning to the courtroom. All of a sudden everything is silent. I'm sure terror is written all over my face. I'm so ashamed to be involved in this charade.

The testimony continued with Vincent Pagglione doing the questioning. "How long have you been with Channel 8, Ms. Clark? I believe you mentioned at the first session -- I believe you said nine years?"

"Yes, and I am hoping to retire with Channel 8. Broadcasting is my life, Mr. Pagglione. Ever since I was a little girl, I dreamed of working in television, and I always have been driven to be a first-class reporter. That dream has come true for me.

As a Court Reporter, I have never experienced anything so brutal. I can see that Rita Clark is beginning to fall apart. Tears are beginning to stream down her face. She has a look of desperation. Goodness, this is so traumatic for her. She is fearful of losing her career. Bless her heart. She is begging the Grand Jurors to understand that she isn't guilty of anything except wanting to protect not only Pit Bulls but all animals from cruelty.

I feel like crying for her. My eyes are beginning to water. I've got

to stop this right now. It is dangerous at this point to show the least bit of sympathy toward Rita Clark or any other person connected to this case.

All of a sudden, to my surprise, Rita Clark blurts out a surprising remark, looking directly at the District Attorneys. "I know for a fact that one of the D.A.'s here in Jefferson County was charged with a wrongful act, but no action was ever taken against him in any way. He was guilty and everyone knew it. If he would have gone to trial he would have been found guilty. He would have lost everything, his profession, his reputation and the final outcome, he would have been disbarred, but his wrongful actions were swept under the carpet, so to speak."

Vincent had a ghastly hateful look on his face.

Rita Clark was somber as she said, "Members of the Grand Jury, I am asking you, pleading with you not to indict me. Please allow me to retain my job, to continue with the profession that I love so much. In fact, I am begging you to take a hard look at the facts and realize that if I made a few mistakes along the way in gathering information for the Pit Bull story that you will understand that I only did it for one purpose, to show the public the cruelty and mistreatment of these animals. Human beings are teaching these wonderful dogs to be killers.

Please, again, I beg you, look at the evidence. Hopefully you will come to the conclusion that I honestly did not have any idea that what I was doing was considered criminal in nature. Again, I repeat, please do not indict me. I love my profession and have spent my entire adult life trying to get where I am now, and I hope you will have compassion for me."

I feel tremendous compassion for Rita Clark. Bless her heart. She is sobbing. She is wanting to say something else. Oh my gosh, Vincent is rudely interrupting her. He coldly said: "Ms. Clark, you can step down now. You will be recalled again for further testimony."

I am beside myself. Something I've learned in life from this experience, among others, there are devils in our midst. How Vincent Pagglione can live with himself is beyond me. He exhibits such callousness that is unconscionable and shows no emotion whatsoever.

Rita Clark is holding tight to her attorney, Mr. Bennett. She looks like she is almost staggering out of the courtroom. I can tell they are devastated. Without a doubt, Pagglione is a monster.

A break was taken, and during the twenty minute break there was laughter amongst Pagglione, McCallister, and Summers. Look at that, I thought: They are already acting like winners. I'm in shock. I can't believe what has just transpired. How can they torture Ms. Clark this way? At the same time, I feel like they are torturing me, putting me in jeopardy with my own profession, the way they are manipulating this case.

As far as I am concerned, this is a complete indictment of the system when District Attorneys carry on this way. They are supposed to protect the sanctity of the Grand Jury by never going off the record. I'm angry, scared, and I feel helpless.

The break is over. Pagglione is introducing the videos into evidence, and they are playing them for the Grand Jurors. These videos were shown to the public. All four segments were shown on Channel 8 during high rating times. Well, I thought: The District Attorneys don't want to leave anything to the imagination. They are bound and determined to get an indictment from the Grand Jurors by trying to prove Rita Clark is guilty on all counts, and they are pushing beyond the limits of the Grand Jury Rules to make sure her career is ruined forever.

This is gruesome, the way they hang the Pit Bulls on clotheslines and teach them all kinds of vicious ways to prepare them to go into battle and fight until one wins and the other bleeds to death. These dogs are innocent in the beginning. After their torturous training, they end up to be killers. Blood Sport they call it.

The session finished at 12:30 a.m. at which time I felt like screaming. I'm going to leave this toxic environment as quickly as I possibly can. No courtesy is shown to me anymore as far as making sure I safely leave the courthouse and safely get to my car.

Vincent Pagglione is approaching me. I'd sure like to tell him what I think, but I'm too fearful of the outcome.

"Allison," he said in an arrogant tone, "The transcript from this evening needs to be on my desk Thursday morning." I am so disgusted that Vincent Pagglione didn't even ask if that would be okay or possible. I answered, trying to keep my cool, "Sure thing." Vincent Pagglione has such a satisfied smile on his face, and said, "Fine then," and he swaggered from the courtroom without another word.

The Rita Clark case continued on every Tuesday and Thursday for several more weeks, and the District Attorneys dragged every known witness they could think of to the stand to testify about this alleged crime that Rita Clark and the videographers had committed.

CHAPTER 17

On July 15th, I held my breath, hoping the session wouldn't last long. I am packed and looking forward to Sarah's arrival. I am looking forward to driving to Estes Park. It is so beautiful. All I keep thinking about is sitting through the replay of these Pit Bulls being viciously trained and tortured to learn to fight to kill their opponents which is pure agony for me.

I notice that some of the Grand Jurors are covering up their eyes or turning away in certain portions of the video. Finally the session is over which has lasted for two heartbreaking hours, and everyone has been excused and left the courtroom. I am able to pack up and leave the courthouse without Vincent approaching me.

The following morning the alarm rang at 6:00 a.m. I knelt by my bedside and said my prayers. Then I got ready to go pick up Sarah at the Denver International Airport. Sarah was standing on the curb when I arrived. I got out of my vehicle and ran towards her.

"Sarah. How are you? Give me a big hug, sweetheart." Sarah kissed me on the cheek and tightly hugged me.

"It is so wonderful to see you, Allie."

"You look great Sarah, as usual. You are so beautiful."

"Why thank you, Allie." When we arrived at the townhouse and entered the great room, I teasingly asked Sarah, "How do you like my painting? A very well- known artist gave this to me. Don't you think it is magnificent?" Sarah laughed and shook her head. "Yes, it is. It is magnificent."

"Allie, you look a bit thinner than usual. I can tell you are not getting enough sleep. This trip will definitely do both of us some good. I am going to insist that you sleep in Saturday and Sunday morning. Your mother would be worried sick if she knew that you weren't taking care of yourself. Now, I have ground rules for you. You are not to talk about your job, nothing negative. Do you hear me? You are to rest and enjoy, and I mean that."

"Yes ma'am. Let me just give Meg a call and give her some instructions. I am almost ready to go. Hey, grab whatever you would like to drink or eat out of the refrigerator. First I want to show you something before we go. Better yet, while I'm talking to Meg, please step into the bedroom and look around. When I finish the call, you can tell me what you think."

Sarah grabbed a water out of the fridge and headed straight for the bedroom.

"Sarah, I'm back. Meg isn't home right now. I'll have to touch base with her later."

"Allie, this is a beautiful guest bedroom. You have impeccable taste. The earth colors are soothing."

"How do you like the brass canopy bed?"

"Wonderful. I think King Size is practical, and the bedspread and gargantuan pillows are gorgeous. You have decorated your townhouse so warm and comfortable. It gives one the feeling of never wanting to leave, Allie."

"Thank you so much."

I could curl up in that bed right now, and you would have trouble ever getting me out again."

"I'm glad you like it, Sarah. I had a lot of fun decorating the room."

"You know, Allie, I'll have to be honest with you. Your entire townhouse looks like it came out of Better Homes and Gardens."

"Sarah, I'll take that as a compliment coming from you. Let's have a prayer, grab our bags and be off. I would like to get into Estes Park before dark." We are so fortunate that it is a gorgeous day. I call it the perfect Colorado day. Look at the blue sky. It is crystal clear. We are going to have so much fun staying again at the Stanley Hotel or as some call it, the Haunted Hotel."

"I am so excited to be here with you, Allie. When have we not had fun together?"

"Isn't that the truth." We both laughed.

As Sarah and I drove away from the City and began to get closer to Estes Park, the fragrance of the air became purely delicious. We sang along with the Beatles. Both of us were beginning to relax.

"Sarah, don't you just love the Aspen trees? The trees are dressed up in full bloom with their leaves shimmering in the breeze."

"Yes, Allie. They are exquisite. I marvel at the various colors of green foliage. Actually, Allie, when I am in the mountains, I feel renewed. I am especially partial to Colorado and Utah because of the beautiful mountain scenery. When I can take my easel and paints into the mountains, I feel like I never want to leave, but I didn't bring them this time, as if you hadn't noticed. I will be packing them when we go skiing in Park City at Thanksgiving. I want to sketch the mountains around Park City in all their majesty.

"Sarah, I think you would feel empty-handed without your sketch pad. Park City is so charming, truly unique, and I insist that you sketch the historic courthouse for me. It's located on Main Street. Would you be willing to do that for me while we are there?"

"What do you think? I would love to do that for you, Allie."

"Thank you so much."

"Have you noticed, Allie, as we get closer to Estes Park, the rock formations begin to appear? The scenery around Estes Park is breathtaking."

"It is definitely one of my favorite places."

I have to be cautious. I'm not going to burden Sarah with all the clutter going on in my head. I'm trying my hardest to not think about the horrific situation I am in. I know I need to do everything in my power to leave everything behind and just enjoy the moment which is becoming much more difficult.

Sarah, on the other hand, was waiting for the right moment to tell Allie what she had hidden in her heart, a secret. I'm definitely going to wait until Monday morning when Allie is more rested.

We spent a glorious weekend in Estes Park, and on Sunday after a wonderful breakfast we headed toward Longs Peak.

"Sarah, I would like to get at least a four-hour hike in on Longs Peak. Maybe we can if we are lucky."

"That would be great, Allie."

When Sarah and I returned from the hike, I shouted, "I feel exhilarated. The scenery is breathtaking. I'm so happy that you painted the Aspen trees of Longs Peak for me. I will treasure that painting forever. I love this area."

Sarah still was on guard about talking to Allie about her secret. She was waiting for just the right moment: I think Monday morning is the best time.

On Sunday morning they found a Mormon Branch of The Church of Jesus Christ of Latter-day Saints. They quietly walked in to attend sacrament meeting. They did not want to miss partaking of the sacrament.

"You know, Sarah, I feel so much better. Sacrament meeting was wonderful. The testimonies seemed especially genuine. It's so important that we remember our Savior and the atonement, what he sacrificed for us. I love the Savior with all my heart and soul."

"Allie, your example has been what has held me together during rough times, and your mother has the most beautiful testimony I've ever heard. Your whole family gives me the desire to live more righteously."

"Sarah, that is a wonderful compliment. I appreciate your saying that. I've always felt fortunate for mother and daddy and their example to all of us kids while we were growing up.

I want to say in all sincerity that this trip to Estes Park is more than I had hoped for, Sarah. It is so enjoyable to be with you."

"I feel exactly the same way, Allie."

"We traded off driving back to my condo. I could tell that Sarah enjoyed driving my Ford Mustang. When we got back home, we got ready for bed, sat on the deck for a half an hour and talked.

"Allie, I can't wait to try out your new King-Size bed." Sarah said to herself: This still is not the time to tell Allie. Tomorrow morning I'll break the news.

After a light breakfast on Monday morning, Sarah waited for the right moment. "Allie, how about grabbing another cup of herbal tea, and we will sit on the deck. I want to talk to you. I've waited for the right moment to break this news. I hope you are ready for this."

I was curious and somewhat apprehensive. I replied, "What Sarah?"

"Well, Allie, it is about Todd."

"What about Todd? I am not sure I want to go there."

"Allie, it has been difficult for me to approach you regarding this, but now is as good a time as ever, and I think you are pretty much over him now."

"Well, Sarah, to be totally honest, I can't say that for certain. I'll never forget all the wonderful memories. I was deeply in love with Todd, and every time I go on a date I compare the guy with Todd. What happened? Did Todd get married? Whatever it is, I guess it is best you tell me. Shoot."

"Well, I saw Todd a couple of months back. I ran into him at the Mall."

How is he doing? I wish him well, no matter what. Now I am dying of curiosity, Sarah. Has he been convicted of a crime or what?"

Sarah chuckled. "Not hardly."

I can't help but notice that Sarah is trying to be as tactful as possible. She knows how frail I am.

"Allie, he looked terrible. In fact, he has lost weight. He had circles under his eyes. You could tell he was in a depression. He was not himself at all. First of all, I need to tell you that when I spotted him at the Mall, I was shocked. The truth is, I wasn't sure it was him. He looked so different. When I approached him, and heaven knows why I did that, he recognized me, and I am convinced he was trying to get away, trying to avoid me."

"Sarah, that doesn't sound like the Todd I once knew and loved. What in the world has been going on with him, Sarah?" My heart sank.

"Well, Allie, first of all I'm not supposed to be telling you this. He swore me to secrecy, but I feel you deserve to know the truth, and maybe you will better understand why he hurt you so severely."

I remained silent, and I know down deep I am afraid of the truth. I hung on to every word Sarah was saying.

"Todd was so surprised to see me, Allie. I could tell he felt so guilty. He hugged me and then began to cry. I was, needless to say, feeling bad for him instead of anger towards him. We both decided we needed privacy to talk. We found an area in the Mall that was deserted.

Okay. When Todd returned from his mission in Brazil, his family and friends were at the airport. They were cheering him on as he stepped off the plane. Your absence was noticeable, of course, as well as mine. He told me that his mother and dad had decided, right at the end of his mission, that they had met the most wonderful girl who had moved into their ward from California, Molly Jo, and they were convinced that he would think so too. So Molly Jo was at the airport to greet him, even kissed him on the cheek.

Todd said that he was uncomfortable about the whole set-up. He didn't quite know how to react. He said his parents were elated. They told Todd that they did love you, Allie, but they did not think you were the one for their son. They felt that Molly Jo would be more suited for Todd, because they both were interested in studying law, not to mention that Molly Jo happened to come from a lot of money, lots, on both sides of the family. So in a sense they bribed Todd to date her, offering to pay full tuition for his Law School at the University of Utah.

Todd admitted to me that guilt overcame him at times, especially because over all this time he hadn't contacted you. In his heart he wanted to be truthful with you and tell you the circumstances. As time passed, he began to realize what a jerk he had been. Then he became too fearful to talk to you. His parents suggested that not talking to you or seeing you again was the right thing to do. He admitted to me that over time he was dying inside of guilt.

Anyway, he dated Molly Jo, kissed her two or three times over a period of six months, but began to know in his heart that he did not like her, not one iota, and he did not think he had a thing in common with her. Todd began to have the opinion that Molly Jo was a first-class snob. He said she dressed very stylish, and was without a doubt beautiful, but he felt that she didn't possess any of the qualities that you have, Allie.

At that point in the conversation, he began to sob, and you won't believe it, Allie. I was sobbing right along with him.

"Sarah, I am going to grab us some bottled water."

"Sure. Thank you for the water. Do you want me to continue?"

"Yes. Oh, yes. I need to know for my own sanity."

"Well, the conversation with Todd got more emotional as we sat there. He told me that there is no one in this whole world that he has loved like he loves you. His life has been one big roller coaster ride since he returned from his mission."

I couldn't help but smile, thinking: Join the crowd, Todd.

"Allie, he hesitated to go into detail about everything, but he wanted me to know also that there was no way he could ever have tried to make contact with you, because he was so ashamed of himself. He and his parents are not on speaking terms these days. He is having a difficult time trying to forgive them, and he blames them for the fact that he lost you."

"Honestly, I don't know what to think. One part of me wants to hate him but, Sarah, you know I don't believe hating anyone is the answer to our problems. It certainly is not our Savior's teachings. You know how much I loved him, and as odd as this may sound to you, I still do."

"Yes, I know."

I know that Sarah is being very careful and patient with me. Bless her heart. She patted me on my back a few times. Now she is being so quiet, more than likely to give me a chance to grasp the situation. A short time passed and then I said with sincerity, "Sarah, I feel numb, but confused as to where to go from here." Then I began to laugh. My laughter set Sarah off, and she began to laugh nervously.

"Allie, you cannot believe how relieved I am that I finally have told you. It has been on my mind and bothering me for a long time. Allie, I feel that, for some reason, you will be alright now."

"You know, Sarah, I feel relieved as well. My heart aches for Todd, but I'm going to have to take some time to decide whether I should try to help him or not. I've been so devastated and hurt from the beginning when he didn't even call me that I think the only thing I should do now is to allow time to go by and hope for the best."

"One other very important thing is, Allie, I swore to Todd that the conversation we had would be kept secret. Todd will never trust me again if he ever finds out that I told you. Keep in mind, he poured his heart out to me and, as you know, for a man that is extremely difficult to do. Promise me that whatever you do, whether you see Todd again or not in the future, you will never tell him what I have told you today."

"I promise, Sarah. Crazy as this may sound, I'm happy to know that Todd still loves me. I'm pretty sure that I'll never meet up with him again in this life. I could be wrong, but I doubt it."

"Well, Allie, you have to admit Todd has such a wonderful personality. I understand completely why you fell in love with him."

"Yes. I did fall in love with him, but I'm sure now that I must have been naive regarding Todd. I'm somewhat disappointed that he didn't stand up to his parents and tell them what he wanted instead of caving in when they put pressure on him. Maybe I'm being too harsh."

"You know, Allie, he has suffered."

"What do you mean?"

"Well, he told me all about what had happened to him. His folks kept writing letters to him while he was in Brazil, bragging and talking to him about how wonderful Molly Jo's parents are and how beautiful Molly Jo is and enticing him in other ways as well. They told him they would buy him a car when he got home, but as he said, there were strings attached, namely Molly Jo.

He is still deeply in love with you, Allie. You need to know that. You also need to know that he felt stricken with fear that he could possibly run into your parents. He said that he loves your parents to this day, your whole family for that matter, and the way he handled everything gave him such a tremendous feeling of regret and shame that he felt he could never face your parents again.

He has been accepted at the University of Utah Law School, but to me he seems burned out, not knowing really what to do with his future. He feels like he betrayed you in so many ways which, in fact, he did."

"Let's face it, Sarah, honesty is always the best policy. When you hide things, especially from someone you love, you keep digging a hole deeper and deeper. It is a travesty the way we have both had to suffer because Todd was not able to come forward and talk everything over with me. The way I see it, maybe we could have worked our relationship out down the road. Maybe. I can assure you of one thing, Sarah. Todd needs to forgive his parents. They are good people even if they chose Molly Jo over me. Being hateful to his mother and dad is too heavy of a burden for anyone.

I know mother and daddy were so devastated when Todd rejected me, and none of us could figure it out, but I can tell you to this day that down deep they love Todd Lewis as if he were their own son. They have taught me not to harbor hateful feelings about other people, and, of course our Savior is the best example of teaching us to love even our enemies. I have to admit, Sarah, that it is difficult to have good feelings toward wicked people, especially when people are dishonest or crude right before your eyes."

"Yes, Allie, I agree with that."

"I have to admit also, Sarah, that Todd did make all of our lives fuller. He was so much fun to be with, and I don't regret a moment of our relationship. He's a great guy, and I don't want him to continue suffering. Sarah, we need to move on now, all of us."

"Allie, no wonder he loved you so much and still does. Believe you me, he cried when he told me how much he adores you and how much he loves you still, but he doesn't really think you will ever forgive him."

"Sarah, I'm going to have to take my time. Right now the pressure of work is getting me down. I need to take one day at a time and finish this Grand Jury case and go from there. I don't think for now it would be good for either of us to renew our relationship or if ever. Todd deserves happiness. Heaven knows, I am sure he has suffered more than me. I just wish he would have been honest with me then, come clean, but now that I know about all that happened to him, I can understand more fully how difficult that would have been for him at the time."

"Changing the subject, I hate to leave you, Allie. We have had such a wonderful time in Estes Park, but we can look forward to skiing, to our heart's content, the slopes of Park City. If all goes well, maybe your family would be interested in spending a day at the Hot Springs in Midway."

"I'm sure they would, Sarah. That's a must to put on the agenda. Sarah, I am so glad you came. I have to tell you, I will feel lonesome when you leave. You can't beat old friends. You know me like no one else does."

"Well, Allie, I look forward to great times ahead, and I know one day both of us will find some nice guys to settle down with and have a family. I want that more than anything else in the world."

"Yes. I would love that too, Sarah. Sarah, on the serious side, if anything did happen to me, I would like you to have my car. You seem to like it a lot."

"That is silly. Nothing is going to happen to you. Why are you talking like that? You are way too young to die. Don't scare me like that. You are not suicidal, are you?"

"Heavens no. I am not suicidal. I hope I am not sounding silly, but you never know. Anyway, I have thought about it lately, you know, if I should drop over dead with exhaustion or slip on a piece of soap in the tub. I definitely want mother to have all of my jewelry except the friendship diamond ring that Todd gave me. I guess I should have given the diamond ring back to Todd long ago, but I never wanted to see him again."

Sarah shook her head in disbelief. "Allie, are you crazy? I always thought people talked about dying when they reached 75 or 80."

"Maybe it sounds crazy to you, Sarah, but I have thought a lot about it lately."

I cannot tell Sarah my true feelings; that I fear for my life; that sometimes I feel that someone is following me; that I leave the courthouse feeling terrified on some of the evenings and early morning hours; that what Rosie said to me has bothered me since it occurred; that Vincent Pagglione treats me so disrespectful; that he is going off the record in the Grand Jury proceedings and, unbelievable even to me, that I am going along with their criminal activities. I feel like I am an accomplice.

Turning to the Lord and asking Him in humility to protect me is the only comfort I get. I know within my heart that without the Lord in my life I would have never made it this far.

"Sarah, let's change the subject about death. You have only got such a short time left to be here. Let's get back on track with some positive thoughts. How about soaking in the hot tub and forgetting all of this negative stuff for a bit. I apologize for talking about death. I guess it is a bit silly. Anyway, you won't hear it from my lips again. Okay?"

"You promise, Allie? If you mention it again, I'm going to cover my ears. Allie, if you feel like you are sinking into a depression or need me, I am just a phone call away. You have the love and support of your family, and you know I'll always be there for you. I know I'm repeating myself, but will you promise me that you will ask for help if you need it?"

"I promise, Sarah. When did you say the cab is arriving to take you to the airport?"

"They will pick me up at six o'clock."

"Now I am repeating myself, but you know I will gladly take you to the airport."

"Yes, but why? You need to rest and then I guess you are going to have to work nonstop until October. Please, whatever you do, don't neglect yourself. Eat a high protein diet, drink plenty of water, and you need at least eight to nine hours of sleep a night. Are you listening to me?"

"Yes. Sarah, you are beginning to sound like my mother. The truth is, the tension I am experiencing in this Grand Jury case has caused me to doubt myself as to what I can handle and not handle. I'd be lying if I didn't tell you the truth. This case is grueling. It is wearing me down."

"Allie, I know you. You are a survivor. There is no doubt about that. Anyway, the hot tub sounds inviting."

"Sarah, one of the commandments is that we must endure to the end. That's what I have to always remember.

How about a glass of V8 Juice, crackers and, your favorite, Sharp Cheddar Cheese?"

"Sounds more than good to me."

"Sarah, the time has flown by. I'm glad we had this time together. It felt good to laugh and cry to our heart's content. We are definitely made out of the same cloth when it comes to showing our emotions. Actually, I feel better right now than I have in months. This break has been therapeutic."

"Allie, I wouldn't have wanted to miss this weekend for anything. Nature revitalizes the soul. I better get myself ready to go. I want you to see my new slack outfit. How do you like it?"

"Absolutely stunning, Sarah.

The moment has come. Brewster called me and told me the cab is waiting for you out in front. Let me help you with your bags. Oh, Sarah, give me a big hug. Thank you for coming. I love you for just being you."

"Allie, don't cry. I can't cry or I'll ruin my makeup."

Tears were shed by me when Sarah left in the cab. I threw her a kiss and waved to her as she turned the corner. Sarah gave me one last wave, and then she was gone.

I had such a great time with Sarah. Already I feel am emptiness in the pit of my stomach. Talking about Todd shocked me in some ways but also made me yearn for the good old days we had together. He still loves me.

The way everything turned out between us makes me feel sad. Why am I feeling so isolated? It's more than likely because I don't have Todd in my life anymore, and I can't confide to anyone about what is going on in the Grand Jury sessions. I'll be sure to write in my journal. It is helping somewhat. I find it necessary to write about the details.

Sarah thinks I'm crazy when I bring up the subject of death, but none of us know how long we will journey on this earth. I think I show love if I am thoughtful enough to tell my loved ones what they should do with my assets in case of my death. I hate to admit it, but I am becoming morbid in some ways.

CHAPTER 18

On Tuesday morning, July 19th, I dressed in my jogging outfit, drove to the bank with a four-page will and had it notarized by a Notary Public. I signed the documents along with two witnesses. They each put their initials on all four pages.

I feel better now that my will is completed. I drove away from the bank with the idea in mind that I am going to make three copies, one for my safe deposit box, one for Meg, and one for my file.

Now I need to stop at Meg's house to talk to her about this will. I hope she doesn't think I am crazy. I look forward to seeing her. I rang her doorbell. Meg answered the door immediately.

"Allie, how have you been? How was your trip to Estes Park?"

"It was great. Sarah is a joy to be with, and we both needed a break in the worst way."

"It was well deserved. Allie, it seems like you have been working twenty-four seven. If you don't slow down, you could end up the richest girl in the graveyard."

"I definitely am going to slow down after this Grand Jury case is completed, Meg. You may as well plan to take a break yourself when I do, and then we will both be refreshed. I owe you a lot for how efficient you have been with all the rush transcripts we have worked on."

"Allie, you are so kind. Of course, Allie, I know we are not to discuss the case, but just one comment."

"What is it that you want to say?"

"From proofing these transcripts, I have to admit to you that this case seems unbelievably strange."

"Isn't that the truth? Oh well. Look at it this way, Meg. We are making good money. Just between you and me, I am not enjoying working on this case at all. I cannot wait until we finish."

"I can see why you would feel that way."

"I guess we have said enough about that. Now, Meg, I came over here to see you for an important reason."

"And what would that be?"

"Well, Meg, please don't think I am crazy."

"Honey, anybody who is in this profession has to be somewhat crazy. Wouldn't you agree?"

"You said it. I didn't." We both laughed heartily. "Anyway, Meg, I have something for you."

"What is this?"

"Promise you won't laugh?"

"I promise, Allie."

"It's my Last Will and Testament."

"Allie, you have got to be kidding? Wouldn't you say you are a bit too young to worry about wills?"

"I feel that I'm being practical. Meg, please don't look at the will now. Just keep this copy in your files. I mean, you can look at it, if necessary, upon my death. That will be the end of it, okay?"

"What do you mean, the end of it?"

"I mean, we don't have to discuss it any further than this and you know me, Meg, I always like to be prepared for anything that might happen. I could be killed going to work this evening. It's better that I protect my assets."

"I understand. If I had any common sense, I should probably prepare a will as well. To be perfectly honest with you, I have never thought about it, but you are right. Anything can happen."

"Meg, I better go. I have got some last minute things I want to take care of before Grand Jury tonight. Geez, my anxiety level is already beginning to rise."

"Try the best you can, Allie, to stay calm. By the way, thanks for the work. It has kept me from going bankrupt. If I complain, just ignore me. I don't mean it most of the time."

"Listen, Meg, if I couldn't bounce off you once in a while, who knows where I could end up."

"Allie, you are a character, you know that? I am just joking."

Laughing I said, "I don't think I know much of anything anymore, Meg, except I know I better get going. You will be hearing from me tomorrow. Thanks again for being so helpful."

"Sure. Talk to you tomorrow, Allie.

"Take care, Meg."

"Thanks for stopping by."

"You bet." I am feeling anxious. I need to talk to Sarah as soon as I get home to make certain she arrived home safely. As soon as I arrived home and took care of some business details, I called Sarah."

"Sarah speaking."

"Sarah, how was your flight home?"

"Oh, Allie, it was bumpy. I get nervous when there is too much turbulence. Anyway, thank you for asking. I am safely home. One thing for sure, after such a wonderful weekend, it is going to be somewhat difficult to get back to reality. I am convinced that there are times when I like to be terribly lazy."

"I hear you. Sarah, hold on a minute. My timer on the stove is going off." Sarah is feeling guilty because Todd called her and asked her about Allie. She knew if Allie knew that, it would not be good. Sarah did not want Allie to ever think that she would do anything behind her back, but Todd wanted desperately to know how Allie was getting along and if she was still as beautiful as she used to be.

Sarah had to remind Todd of her long-time friendship with Allie, and that it was better if he did not call her again. She did not want to hurt his feelings. She told him that she loved him and wished him the best for his future. She could tell by his voice that he was distraught. She knew Allie would have compassion for him.

"Okay, Sarah, I'm back. I've got to go tie up some business. I love you Sarah and look forward to our family vacation together. We'll have a ball."

"Yes, we will. Love you, Allie."

"Bye-bye." I better get ready for Grand Jury.

I seem to be the first one arriving for the session. I still can't get over how rude Vincent Pagglione is becoming towards me. The only problem is that not only is Pagglione rude towards me, but now McCallister and Summers are becoming more unfriendly every time we meet. I am just going to have to ignore it as much as I possibly can and concentrate on doing my job.

Written transcripts were handed out to all of the Grand Jury members regarding when Willy, who was wired to the hilt, entrapped Rita Clark, and was successful in doing so, getting her to talk candidly, and the conversations between the two of them were typed up for each Grand Jury member to have a copy.

I could not help from smiling when I thought about Rita Clark and how she can swear like a drunken sailor. She made some comments that made me want to cringe. I admit that sometimes it is almost impossible to control my emotions. People do say some of the craziest things. I have to constantly be on guard. I have to keep telling myself to practice self-control. I don't want the Grand Jurors to see me laughing or crying.

The transcripts were read by the Grand Jurors as they listened to the audio tapes of Rita Clark speaking which were played at the same time, and then they called one of the T.V. reporters, David Burke, to the witness stand. His testimony lasted for three hours. Again, I am getting tired of the repetition. I'm sure that the Grand Jurors are becoming worn out or bored. I see that a few of them are dozing off.

I can't even be too friendly with the Grand Jurors anymore, and I have to use a bathroom on another floor so that I won't accidentally meet up with Rosie. Rosie seems like she is in her glory. She acts like she is enjoying the case more than anybody else. She asks more questions of the witnesses than anybody.

I still am not sure what her role is in all of this, but without a doubt she was called to be a Grand Juror for a specific purpose. I will still avoid her, no matter what.

The next Grand Jury session came quicker than I could believe. The witness for that evening was the producer of the Channel 8 television station. His testimony dragged on for four and a half hours. The entire month of July was more of the same thing, endless witnesses talking about absolutely nothing that the Grand Jurors hadn't heard over and over and over again.

I am worn to a frazzle. I can't imagine how many more witnesses can testify to the same thing. These guys are totally out of hand. Well, at least my pockets are jingling.

In reality, though, I feel self-hatred, frustration, fear, and a lot of guilt for not being able to speak up. Although, the worst part of all of this is, speak up to whom? I can't put my finger on exactly who is in on this conspiracy. If I didn't know any better, I'd say that the D.A.'s and the investigators are all in this together. They are like pariahs, all fawning and gravitating toward Vincent Pagglione.

CHAPTER 19

"On August 5th, I drove into the parking lot at the courthouse and, as usual, packed up my equipment and headed for the entrance trying to convince myself that I am ready for another Grand Jury session My only hope is that this case will be completed in October.

Oh no, here comes Chief Judge Zacharelli. I wonder what in the devil he wants.

"Hi Allison. How are you this evening?"

For some reason, the Judge doesn't seem his old boisterous self.

"Hi Judge. I'm well, thank you. And you?"

"Good enough. Allison, I need to speak with you for a few minutes. Do you have time?"

"Sure, Judge."

"Why don't you get your equipment set up and then meet me in my chambers, and we can chat."

"Okay. That will be fine."

"I'll see you shortly then."

My stomach is beginning to hurt, and I feel dizzy and nauseous. What would he want to speak to me about? Please, Lord, help me. I need to settle down. The more I anticipate what this is about, the sicker I'm feeling. Hopefully it is insignificant and doesn't have anything to do with the present Grand Jury case. I actually am beginning to feel like a caged animal the longer this case goes on. I can't turn to anyone. The major problem being, I don't know who I can trust.

Keep your mouth shut. Speak when spoken to. Stay in control, whatever you do.

When I arrived at the entrance to the Judge's chambers Judge Zacharelli met me there. He spoke loud. "Come on in, Allison." I'll be back shortly."

Judge Zacharelli looks larger every time I see him. His hair needs cutting. It's so bushy. That mustache of his needs a trim, and those large eyeglasses with his small piercing brown eyes that look straight at me can be intimidating, even evil. His ego is difficult to describe. I know the Judge well. He can rattle the attorneys with his booming voice. I've noticed that particular attorneys that the Judge dislikes, when they come to the podium to speak, their legs shake or their hands shake uncontrollably. It is a well-known fact that the Judge has a loud mouth. We can hear him out in the hallway from quite a distance, either laughing hysterically or yelling at someone. He has a terrible temper. I've seen him, on occasion, crack the whip.

I wonder why it is taking the Judge so long to return. I smell a scent of smoke in his chambers. Nothing surprises me anymore. I know from rumors, not really catching him in the act myself, but that he often smokes behind closed doors. Oh boy, I have reason to believe the rumors now. His ashtray reveals the telltale sign, and a janitor didn't sweep up the ashes on the floor carefully enough. Shame on you Judge Zacharelli. Disgusting. Being he is the Chief Judge, he should know that smoking in the courthouse is totally against all Rules, and in case he doesn't know it, I should remind him that that means even the hierarchy.

I hate to think it, but the Judge is a slob. Glancing around his chambers, it looks to me like it would be almost impossible to find even the least little thing. When he puts on his robe, he has the same problem. He looks disheveled. I have heard through the grapevine that he has been married three times and has four children between all three marriages. All I can think of is that all three wives were lucky enough to flee from his grips.

He can be a tyrant in many respects. He runs the show and no one questions his authority, ever. I wouldn't even attempt to cross him nor would anyone else I know. Here he comes. I feel like closing my eyes and praying. He even walks in a slothful manner. He entered his chambers and closed the door.

Please, let this be an insignificant issue. He got right to the point. He immediately asked me, "Vinny tells me that you have been working pretty steady lately?"

"Uh-huh." They must be on friendly terms for the Judge to call him "Vinny." It is exactly what I suspected that they were best buddies. "Yes. We have been real busy with this Grand Jury case. It has become quite time-consuming, Your Honor."

"Vinny tells me that you are doing all of the transcripts rush." The Judge is just making small talk, but I can tell that he is anxious to get rid of me. He is trying not to create any suspicion by me. Too late.

"Yes, Your Honor. It has kept me extremely busy."

"I suppose you are wondering why I wanted to talk to you?"

"Yes, Your Honor. I am wondering why."

"Well, I just wanted to remind you of the Grand Jury Secrecy Oath you took upon being sworn in as our Grand Jury Court Reporter. Once in a while it is a good idea to remind people how serious it is in these Grand Jury cases to be sure to not leak any information to anyone. Of course, you realize the importance of the Oath of Secrecy that you took when you began as the Grand Jury Reporter, what, six years ago?"

"Yes, Your Honor." I am furious. I do not know why the Judge has to continue harping on the importance of the Oath of Secrecy. I understand.

"Allison, it is very important that absolutely no information be leaked out of any of these Grand Jury proceedings, and I hope you don't take it lightly, young lady."

I am extremely annoyed. The judge's tone of voice is rising to a high pitch. "Your Honor, I am very cautious about that. I have also made it a point to remind my scopist of the Oath of Secrecy that she agreed to.

"Good. Well, Allison, I don't mean to sound stern, but I will warn you that if any leaks come out of any of the Grand Jury cases, you, as well as anyone participating will be suspect. Do you understand where I am coming from?"

"Well, of course I understand." Only too well. Unfortunately, I also understand now that you, Judge Zacharelli, are a part of this conspiracy. I also understand now that Vincent

Pagglione, Jim McCallister and Morgan Summers are all involved in this dastardly plot to hang Rita Clark. You are all in this together.

"Your Honor, I have never spoken to anyone regarding any Grand Jury case that I have been involved in. I would never put myself in jeopardy regarding the Grand Jury Oath of Secrecy, nor would Meg Sorenson. I have never stepped over the line and talked freely with anyone about the case we are working on now, or for that matter any other case that I have been involved in. You can always count on me."

I'm gasping for air. I need to get out of here.

"Allison, I know we can count on you to follow the Grand Jury Rules." The Judge smirked.

"By the way, Allison, what did you say the name of your scopist is?"

I'm hardly breathing.

"Meg Sorenson."

"Meg Sorenson. How is Sorenson spelled?"

"S-O-R-E-N-S-O-N."

"That will be all. You better be on your way or otherwise you will be late for the Grand Jury session."

"Yes, Your Honor." I now know that I am being watched. I have been used and abused. My nerves are raw. Dear Lord, please help me to pull myself together and to be able to concentrate this evening. This is a frightening mess, but here and now I vow to continue on with courage. Everything will turn out alright if I trust in the Lord.

As I walked into the courtroom, I kept my head up and gave the Grand Jurors a friendly smile. The Grand Jurors were already seated and ready to proceed. Pagglione looked over at me with a disgusted look on his face. I knew he knew where I had been.

The evening dragged on for four hours with two more witnesses testifying and a continuation of more repetition. Finally the session is over. I made it for another round. I feel relieved. As tough as this situation is, for some unknown reason, I feel a sweet spirit surrounding me. Thank you, Lord.

CHAPTER 20

The big bomb will hit for me on August the 10th. My spirits are high.

My thoughts are more positive. Maybe I feel better mentally knowing that this case will be over within a couple of more months. During this session, four witnesses testified. The testimony ended at around midnight.

When the Grand Jury session was over and the Grand Jurors had been dismissed, Pagglione looked in my direction. Oh, no, I muttered. Here we go again. Pagglione is making certain that everyone has left. I am going to be stuck here alone with the devil. Something is brewing. Finally he approached me and in a very abrupt manner said, "Allison, I need you to change some words on some of these transcripts. They are not right. Of course, we understand that you get tired, and with all the rush transcripts you have been doing, we realize at times you probably get in too big of a hurry and make mistakes."

I am fuming. I know my face is red. He's not fooling me one iota. I know that he wants to change the words in the transcripts to bring about the outcome of this case in his favor. How low can this man get? He is bound and determined to make me look incompetent by accusing me of being inaccurate.

I feel as if I could explode. I have to keep saying to myself, Think before you speak. Remember that everyone is on Pagglione's side, and no one will stand behind you under any circumstances.

Take a deep breath. "What do you mean by saying the words are not right on the transcripts?"

"Just what I said," he remarked sarcastically.

"I know I am not perfect, Vincent, but whenever I don't understand words that are being spoken, I try to always ask for the attorney to repeat the question or the witness or whoever is speaking to repeat their words.

What changes are you talking about?" I feel afraid. I need to stand up for myself, but instead I feel as if I am shrinking under the pressure.

"Look, Allison, what you need to do is take this word change list that I have made up for you and make these changes as soon as possible. Do you understand where I am coming from?"

I am stunned. Pagglione has the upper hand, and he knows it. I'm trapped. "Yes, I said shaking, "I understand."

"That a girl. We need your full cooperation in this situation, and I knew you would see how important it is that you make these changes and, of course, we also understand that it's difficult to hear everything during the proceedings, and you are bound to make errors." Pagglione glared at me with hateful eyes.

What a mean spirited remark Vincent Pagglione has made, that I am bound to make errors. I can't believe what he has handed me, three legal sized yellow pages of changes.

"Allison, I will give you back the original transcripts so that you can make the changes on the originals as well. Then you will have to make copies of the pages with the changes on them, and we will insert the changes into the originals and the copies."

I fell silent: I want to be assertive, but I am tongue-tied. Pagglione is asking me now to commit a felony. He's lower than a snake's belly. This goes against everything I've ever been taught in my life. My mother and daddy would not believe in a million years what is happening to me. From the time I was a little girl, my parents taught me how important it is to be honest, and that truth is beauty.

I answered with a whisper, "Sure," If I just had someone I could confide in. I keep questioning why I am not able to stand up for myself. It is plain to see why.   It's them against me, and I am not totally positive who is against me.

I'll get through this. I may feel insecure now, but I know I'm not alone. My Heavenly Father is watching over me, and He will guide me in the right direction.

Altering original transcripts or changing them in any way is a serious crime.

"Okay," Pagglione said with a grin. "I'm glad we are all on the same page. It makes life easier for all of us. You have the word change list with you. Here are the originals. Get these completed and back to me by Thursday. Do not have your scopist make the changes. You do these changes yourself and deliver the transcripts to my office. I know, without saying, that you understand this is confidential?"

"Confidential. I understand."

I am angry. Vincent Pagglione, you are playing with fire, and so am I. I do not understand anything anymore. This is the ultimate betrayal. I am speechless.

"Well, Allison," he said with an arrogant tone of voice, "I have got to get going now. See you on Thursday. Just tell the receptionist that you have an appointment with me when you come in. Do you understand?"

"Sure." What do you want me to say? You'll get your comeuppance one day, Vincent Pagglione.

Pagglione abruptly walked out of the courtroom. I am flushed. My gosh, I am flabbergasted. This case is turning into a nightmare. Now I know I am in a dangerous situation. I feel distraught. I've never been asked to change words on transcripts before. It is a criminal act to tamper with transcripts.

The shocking part of all of this is, I told Pagglione that I would do it by not saying no, or why didn't I tell him to go jump in the lake. I'm not able to think clearly due to fear. Who wouldn't be fearful? I could end up in jail over this.

When I arrived home, I double-locked all of the doors. As I knelt to say my prayers, I wept. I am going to have to force myself to look at the word change sheets, but I'm fearful to even do that. I want to see how drastic these word changes are.

It looks like some of the changes don't really affect the context of the testimonies. It looks like Vincent has used the wrong verb form in some instances, and he wants that changed. This guy is a total perfectionist. He wants to make certain that he is the greatest in his profession; that no one is as articulate as he is; that no one can possibly win as many cases as he can.

I better settle myself down and wait until I get some rest before I can decide what I should do. I am having difficulty going to sleep. I can't stop thinking about what Vincent has asked me to do. It is 4:30 in the morning. I might as well get up. I guess I will go ahead and make the changes. I know that I'm hyperventilating over making these changes. I'm going to have to breathe into a paper bag.

Pagglione and his cronies are beginning to make my life miserable. I'm feeling hatred towards the whole bunch. Oh, no. Some of these changes definitely change the context of some of the testimonies. This throws a whole different light on agreeing to change the words. I feel like a criminal, because I've agreed to go along with Pagglione's request.

Admittedly, from the time I was asked to be the Grand Jury Reporter, I felt it was an honor, and now Vincent Pagglione is jeopardizing my whole career, and I'm going against my own principles in the process. The only way I can go forward is to lean on the Lord for protection. I have faith that in the end all will be well, and when the timing is right I'll be prompted to proceed and do what is right.

I am weary, but I have completed the word changes on the original transcripts and made copies, and on Thursday I will deliver them to Pagglione's office.

Upon arrival at Vincent's office, I told the receptionist that I had an appointment with Vincent Pagglione. The receptionist took me to his office and offered me a seat. Pagglione was on the phone, ready to hang up. I looked around the office and then observed Pagglione sitting there in his executive leather chair and thought to myself that he is such a pompous ass. I'm too angry to be amused. I can't help it.

His office is perfect. Nothing is out of place. It is so sterile.

Pagglione hung up the phone and immediately began to speak. "Allison, thanks for being prompt. I knew you would be."

"You bet." Now I'm without words again being in Pagglione's territory, and I feel uncomfortable waiting for the next bomb to drop. I wonder what he has in mind for me to do next.

"Allison, I just wanted to mention again, this is highly confidential. Do you understand?"

Here we go again.

"Do you understand?"

Pagglione, you must think I'm an idiot. "Yes, I understand." I am dumfounded. Please tell me this is not happening.

"We may need some more word changes on the transcripts as we go along, Allison. I will let you know if that occurs and, of course, as we have already discussed, we need your complete cooperation. Do you understand?"

Please, quit repeating yourself. My head aches. Honestly, Pagglione, I understand only too well. Something else I fully understand as well. You are enjoying this, aren't you? You are loving watching me squirm in my seat with the look of death on my face.

Pagglione sat there thinking that after all was said and done, Allison did end up being the perfect candidate. They did not made a mistake. She will do anything we want her to do.

Meekly, I spoke, "I understand." I understand that I want to get out of here. I feel miserable. I need to talk to Sarah. I stood up to leave and felt dizzy.

"See you this evening Allison."

I can hardly look at Vincent or respond. He's smiling again. That smile of his is the smile of a devil.

"Okay."

Pagglione escorted me out, and I drove home in tears and being overwhelmed with troubling thoughts.

Pagglione, on the other hand, let out a loud roar of delight and celebrated his success by lighting up an expensive Cuban cigar, and then he made a telephone call.

Immediately when I arrived home, I called Sarah.

"Sarah."

"Allie, is that you?"

"Yes, it's me."

Sarah's heart leaped. She thought to herself that for some reason Allie didn't seem like herself anymore. She couldn't understand what was happening to her. "You sound different, Allie. Maybe you are catching a cold or something."

"Sarah." I began sobbing.

"What in the world is the matter?"

"I think I am just a bit tired of this Grand Jury case. The constant demand for rush transcripts is getting to me. I will be alright." I would love to confide in Sarah and tell her everything. From this day forward, I'm going to have to make major changes. I'm not going to allow these wicked creeps to ruin my life.

Sarah felt Allie's pain, and when she heard Allie still crying in the background it made her frantic.

"Listen, Allison Smith. After this case is over, I think you better cool it for a while. Take a break. You are wearing yourself to a frazzle physically and mentally. What do you think about that?"

"I wholeheartedly agree with you, Sarah."

"Well, I have never known you to be so miserable. I can't understand what is so serious about this case. All I can say is, it must be of great importance for you to have to rush all the transcripts."

"Yeah, Sarah. It's real important for sure." Now I have resorted to lying. What I'd like to tell Sarah is that they are making a mountain out of a molehill. I'm sure it would take some pressure off me if I could confide in Sarah. Unfortunately, the situation seems to be getting worse by the day.

"I shouldn't have called you crying like that, dear friend. I do feel frustrated, and you are the only one I can talk to. I cannot upset the family at this time. I'm sure you are thinking I've lost my sense of humor completely."

"Well, please get it back. I want the old Allie back. We have a lot to look forward to. Just start thinking about the family ski trip, and don't take this case so serious. Can you do that for me?"

"I'm going to try, that's for sure." Oh, Sarah, if only I could tell you how I would give anything not to be in this mess. I'm worried sick about the possibility of going to jail myself for making word changes on the original transcripts. I am scared to death, but I know that I have to keep my mouth shut and try to stay calm.

"Sarah, I won't keep you any longer. I have to get myself together for the Grand Jury session this evening, and don't worry. I feel better just talking to you. I love you."

"I love you too, Allie. Just try to take it with a grain of salt, depend on the Lord, and it will be over in October, you said?"

"Hopefully. I will talk to you soon. Love you."

"Love you, Allie." The minute I hung up, mother called.

"Oh, mother, it's good to hear your voice. I miss you and daddy so much."

"Honey, we miss you too. Allie, guess what?"

"I can't guess, mother." I'd like to say, I can't even think straight anymore, mother.

"Lydia just delivered a healthy baby boy. They named him Timothy. She wanted you to be the first to know."

"That's terrific news. How is she feeling? I can't wait to see her and my new nephew."

"She's doing well. The baby weighs eight and a half pounds. He's adorable. I know Lydia misses you terribly. She understands your situation, why you haven't been able to talk to her as often, but she knows that will all change in the near future."

"Well, I can't wait to see all the kids. What a blessing. She has such a beautiful family. I'll bet David and the children are ecstatic."

"Oh, they are. David ran to buy some balloons, and he wanted to call the Bishop and tell him."

"If I were free right now, I would fly home this instant, mother. Well, the only thing that keeps me going is knowing that we will all be together soon."

"Allie, I can't wait to see you. Your daddy says it has not been the same since you moved to Colorado. We have always dreamed of you coming back home, but we realize you have accomplished a great deal and are making a good living."

I think mother would be surprised at how wonderful that sounds, "home." I never thought I would think like this, but I would be more than thrilled to be home and have the comfort of my family surrounding me. I adore them.

"Mother, for sure, I will try to fly home as soon as I get out from under this workload. By the way, how is Mitch getting along with the new girlfriend?"

"Oh, Allie, I think he is falling in love, but we will just have to wait and see. I can't wait for you to meet her and see what you think."

"Mitch has a good head on his shoulders, and I'm confident that he knows what he wants and will be cautious."

"Yes, he does, Allie. Honey, without offering you any advice, be sure to eat well and get enough rest. I'll tell Lydia that you'll travel home as soon as you can. We all love you so much."

"I love you so much as well. Anyway, mother I have to go. I have to get some work done before I go to Grand Jury."

"Allie, you don't seem like yourself. Are you depressed?"

"Sorry if I seem that way mother, but I have got a lot on my mind." Oh, I feel so helpless. I don't want to worry my parents or any of my family for that matter.

"Well, mother, I'll talk to you soon. Love you."

"Okay, Allie. Love you too."

How lucky I am to have such a loving family. I don't know if I could survive without their support. I'm so happy for Lydia. I hope that I will be able to have some children someday. I continue to pray that I will be able to find a loving mate that will take me to the temple to be married and someone who has the desire to have a family like I do.

I am not myself. I seem to be groaning lately. I dread having to go to the Grand Jury session tonight, but I have to be strong now and try to weather the storm. My worst fear is that I may end up with a felony or two myself.

CHAPTER 21

When I arrived that evening in the courtroom, Pagglione treated me like I didn't even exist. He ignored me every chance he got. I glanced over at him, and he gave me a dirty look. Grow up Vincent. You will not get the best of me, try as you may. If I can get hold of myself and think of the humor in all of this, I'm going to be better off. It's all I can do to keep my composure. If looks could kill, I would be dead.

Rosie, for Heaven's Sake, is sitting there with that stupid grin on her face. If all this wasn't so tragic, it would make interesting comedy. I will bet this will be a long session.

Sure enough, I didn't arrive home until 2:30 in the morning. My whole body is aching. I cannot remember ever feeling so exhausted in my entire life. I better check to make sure all the doors are double-locked.

Unbeknownst to Allison, a black shadow appeared outside on her main deck. A man who was dressed in black, quietly snuck around outside her condo, and he passed by the glass double-doors.

We are in the last session for August, and I feel a sigh of relief. I imagine the Grand Jurors will be happy for this case to reach a conclusion. Maybe not Rosie.

Pagglione is giving some closing remarks.

"Members of the Grand Jury. It looks like we might be getting down to the finishing stretch. The way things are going, I would estimate that it won't be more than a month and a half, and we will be finished with the testimony."

The following Tuesday session, Rita Clark was called to testify for the third time. I told myself to relax and take a deep breath.

Rita Clark and her attorney are coming in the courtroom. For some reason, they seem so different than they were on the other two occasions when Ms. Clark testified. Rita Clark has lost that happy go-lucky way about her. Her face is drawn. She looks so serious. Actually, she looks completely worn out. I swear, she has aged ten years. I can relate. I feel like 100 years old. I is unbelievable what stress can do to you.

There stands Pagglione in all his glory with not a scintilla of wear and tear. He appears in rare form. Let the circus begin, Vincent.

"Ms. Clark, I want to remind you that you are still under oath as well as your attorney."

Rita Clark answered humbly. "Yes, sir."

"Ms. Clark, we have called you back here this evening to clear up a few matters." Then the repetition began again. Vincent badgered the poor woman for two hours. Surprisingly, I felt that Rita Clark was handling herself with dignity, considering she had been on the stand for a full two hours of uninterrupted testimony.

I was badly in need of a break.

"Pagglione stated, Ladies and Gentlemen, let's take a brief break." Pagglione must have read my mind. A brief break was taken, and after the break Rita Clark was asked to take the witness stand.

Then all hell broke loose. I was not ready for Rita Clark to express to the Grand Jurors her feelings about the emotional turmoil she has been experiencing. Realizing that she is testifying for the last time before the Grand Jurors, I could sense how bound and determined she was to make sure that she said everything she could possibly say to try to convince the Jurors that if she had known that what she was doing was a criminal offense, she would not have gone forward with the story, but she told the jurors that Channel 8 was 100 percent in favor of her going public with the story, and that the story was broadcast on the air with terrific ratings.

I could see that Pagglione was outraged by Ms. Clark's outburst and he said in a very controlled manner, "Ms. Clark, you need to calm down, please."

Rita Clark, at that point, had had just about enough of Pagglione, and she raised her voice to almost a screaming level. "What are you talking about, Mr. Pagglione? This is my career that's on the line," and then she broke down and began to cry.

I am struggling to hear Rita Clark. Talking and crying at the same time makes it difficult to hear her words. I have to remind myself to focus.

"I have worked my whole life to get to where I am now as a television news reporter, Mr. Pagglione. It is my livelihood as you well know. This is what I dreamed of doing ever since I was a young girl." At this point, Ms. Clark is sobbing so much that no one could hear her. A break had to be taken.

When Rita Clark resumed her seat on the witness stand, Pagglione began firing questions at her, acting callous as usual.

Ms. Clark broke down several times more that evening, and several breaks had to be taken.

I am sickened by the lack of compassion on Vincent's part. In fact, the expressions on the faces of the threesome, Pagglione, McCallister, and Summers look to me like they are enjoying every moment of this charade. You can see that it is pure entertainment for them, not to mention the attention they are receiving from the media.

My heart goes out to Rita Clark. They are throwing daggers at her. My fingers are turning numb, and my brain is turning to putty. The air is filled with tension. I can't believe how they are carrying on. It is absolutely shameful. There is not a doubt in my mind that they are wanting to hang her. What the District Attorneys are doing to this woman is downright harassment. I feel myself wanting to cry. I need to get myself together. Her testimony is dragging on and on. The badgering is ascending to a high level. It is getting downright malicious.

Sinclair Bennett's face is flushed. I can tell that, if he could, he would stand up and read the riot act to Pagglione. I admire him for keeping his composure.

Rita Clark is pleading with the Grand Jurors not to indict her. I have never witnessed anything quite to equal this before. It is agonizing to watch.

Rita Clark is sincere when she says, "Please, I beg you, if you have any compassion for me, please allow me to retain my job. Please. Please don't indict me. With a felony against me, I will never be able to work again in TV broadcasting. I beg you, please understand my situation. If I did something that wasn't quite right, then I apologize." Then she broke down again and started crying so hard that another break had to be taken.

When Sinclair Bennett and Rita Clark and the Grand Jurors left the courtroom, Pagglione, McCallister, and Summers started to laugh. I could hardly bear to look at them. It is difficult enough having to watch Rita Clark beg. Maybe I should find a quiet place to say a prayer. There seems to be no rhyme or reason for any of this deliberate cruelty. It is devilish to treat another human being so unkind. I went to the second floor and prayed.

When I returned to the courtroom, Rita Clark resumed the stand and Pagglione started in again. "Ms. Clark, are you aware of the seriousness of your actions?"

"Mr. Pagglione, I will repeat myself again. What my intentions were, which I can't figure out why it is as serious as you are making it, is to try to inform the public and make people aware that there are a lot of Pit Bulls being trained to be killers, and I don't feel any animal on this earth should have to endure malicious treatment. In fact, as I said before, from what I understand, there are some very affluent people in the Denver metropolitan area who have Pit Bull Rings in their homes. They put these dogs in the ring to fight for sheer entertainment for those present. These people bet on the dogs, hoping that they will have bet on the winner, and they then allow them to fight until one is dead. All I wanted to do is make the public aware of what is going on. Is there a crime in that?

In my opinion, it is these people who are the criminals in the way they torture these dogs, teaching them to be killers.

That is outright cruelty, from any person's standpoint, don't you think?"

I am sure Rita Clark's attorney, Sinclair Bennett, must have said something to her to calm her down. Thank goodness. She seems more in control of her emotions and is fighting back.

"I know of District Attorneys, one being right here in Jefferson County, who have committed far greater crimes than you have brought me here for and, yet, they have been able to continue on with their professions, and none of them were charged with a felony."

I can tell from Pagglione's demeanor that he is furious. "Let's stick to the case we are investigating here in this Grand Jury, Ms. Clark."

It is one o'clock in the morning. They have had Ms. Clark on the witness stand for several hours. Is Pagglione never going to let up? The Grand Jurors look worn to a frazzle.

All of a sudden Rita Clark, without a question being asked by Pagglione, spoke directly to the Grand Jurors. "Please. Please, don't indict me for this. Please allow me to work in my profession. You don't know how much I would appreciate it if you would feel compassion for me and allow me to go forward with my life and my future in the field that I love. I have wanted --"

Vincent, in his arrogant manner, interrupted Rita Clark. "I did not ask you a question, Ms. Clark. You are excused, Ms. Clark, and, again, I want to remind you of the Oath of Secrecy that you have taken, along with your attorney, Sinclair Bennett. Do not discuss your testimony with anyone in or outside of this courtroom. Do you understand?"

"Yes, I understand."

This is excruciating for me. I feel sadness as I watch Rita Clark and Sinclair Bennett gather up their belongings and head for the door. Rita Clark appears weak. Sinclair Bennett is having to almost hold her up as they left the courtroom.

When everyone left the courtroom, Pagglione had the nerve to say to me, "Hey, Allison, how do you think it went tonight?" Then he laughed heartily. I'm so disgusted. I'd like to tell him to go to hell. "Alright, I guess."

Pagglione knows that he has me so terrified at this point that I will do anything he asks me to do. I question my own behavior. He is gloating all over himself. He is chuckling as he packs up and abruptly leaves.

CHAPTER 22

Around ten in the morning, Sarah called me.

"Hi, Allie. How are you?"

"Hanging in there, Sarah. How are you?"

"Fine. I am furiously painting up a storm, getting ready for the New York City Art Fair. I am so excited, Allie."

"I am excited for you."

So what do you think about your new nephew, Timothy, Allie?"

"Isn't it wonderful? Have you gone to see him yet?"

"Yes. Allie he is adorable, and your sister looks wonderful, considering all she has had to go through to bring Timothy into the world."

"Well, to be completely honest, Sarah, I'm 'jealous. I wish it were me."

"I know what you mean. Allie, don't give up. We'll meet someone one day and fall in love, and eventually have a family, I'm sure."

Sarah paused. I don't dare tell Allie that Todd called me a second time, and he asked me all about Allie and how she is doing. I know he is still madly in love with her. She would not like it one bit if she knew that I talked to him. I told him again that it is not good for him to be calling me.

"Sarah, are you there? I hope you are right. It would be wonderful if we both met someone with impeccable character, someone who honors their priesthood. I'm of the opinion they are not out there in the numbers."

"I'd certainly agree with that. Oh, Allie, I wish you were not so tied up and you could come to New York with me in October. We would have a ball."

"Well, that is out of the question. I can't break the continuity. I have promised Pagglione, the District Attorney, that I would be present at every Grand Jury session, and you know me when it comes to commitments. At least I am on the countdown now, and in the meantime we can look forward to our family ski trip and then, can you believe, on January 1st we will be bringing in the New Century?"

"Well, we have an awful lot to look forward to, Allie."

"Anyway, Sarah, this is your big debut in New York, and I want you to knock them dead. Do you hear me?"

"Yes, I hear you and thank you. I am not that confident about myself, but it would be nice."

"You are so talented, Sarah. I am not just saying that because you are my best friend. I am saying that because it is the truth. You are going to go a long way."

"Allie, you always make me feel so good. Even if I don't go a long way, it is nice to have someone who encourages me like you do. It helps, you know. Like your job, painting is a lot of work. It requires a lot of concentration."

"Wait just a second, Sarah. I apologize for interrupting you, but I have another call coming in. I will call you back."

"Okay."

I hope it is not Pagglione. I swear, my heart is pounding.

"Good morning. This is Allison speaking."

"Allison, this is Vincent Pagglione."

"Yes, Vincent. What's up?"

"I need you to pick up some transcripts. There are glaring errors that you have made, and you need to make more word changes."

Now he is accusing me of making glaring errors on the transcripts. I know what he is up to. He's going out of his way to create fear in me. The worst part of it is, I know he is enjoying every minute of it. My throat is dry and I know my voice is raspy.

I responded, "When do you need this done?" I'm all too aware of the dirty rotten tricks you are playing, Vincent, not only on me but with Rita Clark and the videographers. This is incredulous. He is so rude.

"I need you to pick the originals up here in my office in the morning and then deliver them back to me by early afternoon. Okay?"

"Okay."

That was the end of the conversation. Pagglione hung up the phone without saying another word. While he was talking to

Allison, he was in bed at his luxurious condo. When he hung up the phone, he laughed hysterically. He knew full well he had Allison right where he wanted her, scared to death to say no to anything he demanded of her, and that gave him a great feeling of superiority.

I called Sarah back, so horrified I can hardly see straight. Look at me. I am shaking.

"Sarah, hi."

"Allie, who called you, if I might be so nosey as to ask?"

"It was Vincent Pagglione. He's the lead District Attorney on the Grand Jury case, and a number one jerk as well, I might add."

"Some of these District Attorneys are power hungry, aren't they, Allie?"

"That's saying it mildly, but you better believe it. Honey, I have got to hang up. I have to do a favor for this evil guy. I'd like to use stronger words than that to describe him, but I am sorry I have to hang up so suddenly. I will get back to you as soon as I can."

"I understand completely. I love you Allie. Be careful."

"I love you too, Sarah."

When I hung up the phone, I felt myself sinking. I am in utter shock. Allison Smith, you could end up in prison for this. I cannot deny that I'm turning into a basket case, but within my soul I know that I'm being watched over. That helps to alleviate some of the stress. If I couldn't turn to the Lord, I don't know what I would do. There are times now that I feel the sweet spirit of our Savior. It gives me a feeling of peace. I appreciate those moments, especially under these circumstances. I need to always remember the scripture, I will fear no evil.

I arrived in Pagglione's office at 8:30 the next morning to pick up the transcripts. He was at the front desk to meet me and escorted me into his office.

"Prompt as usual, Allison."

Pagglione is deliberately being sarcastic, grinning from ear to ear.

"Yes." I despise him. I'm sorry, Lord, for feeling the way I do about this man. I know I need to repent. In the six years that I have been the Grand Jury Reporter, no one else has ever complained about errors on the transcripts that I prepared. I am furious at what is happening. In the good old days, all I heard from former District Attorneys was praise.

Every time I get around Vincent of late, I am speechless. It's ridiculous, I know. I am torn up inside, and yet I can't seem to say what I feel, such as: Look, Vincent, I am not changing the words in these transcripts, not for you or anybody else but, try as I may, I become this unbelievably blubbering idiot when I am around him.

"Allison, here are the transcripts. I need you to go through these corrections, one by one, and be very careful that you don't miss anything. Correct these today, okay, and deliver them to me by early afternoon. I need them for tonight."

"Sure." I can't understand the hurry. Rewriting the transcripts is becoming Pagglione's forte, and now they need to be expedited as well.

"Okay, Allison, that will be all."

It is obvious that Pagglione wants me to get out of his office now. Well, the quicker the better. He's standing with his arms folded. I get the message loud and clear.

Pagglione is becoming more concerned about Allison, questioning whether she will keep her mouth shut. He is beginning to feel more and more like she can't be trusted.

As soon as the coast is clear, Pagglione picks up his phone and dials Dino who is temporarily living in a remote cabin west of Central City. He is hiding, waiting for word from Pagglione as to when to make his next move.

"Hey, Dino. How are you doing up there all by your lonesome?" Pagglione is feeling distracted.

"Well, boss, I have been waiting patiently for your next call. What's up, Vinny?"

"I have made up my mind that we can't trust this Court Reporter. She will blow it for all of us. She is just too unpredictable to be trusted."

Dino is thrilled at what he is hearing, because it means a million bucks in his pocket. He is secretly hoping that Pagglione won't change his mind about knocking off this Court Reporter. He is accustomed to living the high life and loves every minute of it, but because of his expensive tastes he needs the million dollars more than he wanted to admit.

"So, what do you have in mind, Vinny?"

"I want to wait a bit more. I'll decide on the right time and place, and I will get back to you." Vincent Pagglione smiled wickedly.

"Gotcha. Don't worry about me, Vinny. This pad up here isn't too bad. At least I have running water and electricity."

"Just hang on tight until you get the word from me, Dino. Forget following her home anymore. Don't get near her. Do you understand? Wait for my instructions. I don't want you or anybody else throwing us a curve. Got it?"

"Gotcha, boss. Yeah."

Pagglione hung up the phone and congratulated himself on how well everything was going. He was bound and determined not to take a chance on Allison opening her big mouth. Besides, being a District Attorney for him was just a stepping stone for better things. He was seeking higher ground like, for instance, running for Congress or the Senate. He felt his future couldn't be brighter. He kept telling himself over and over that: It is just a matter of time.

I did not think that the situation could get worse. Vincent is evil. I've got to get home quickly to work on these changes. The thought of changing some of the words in the transcripts are driving me crazy. I'm feeling more desperate all the time.

When I arrived at my condo, I checked my phone messages. Meg has left me a message. Good. She will deliver the Grand Jury transcripts from the Tuesday night session.

When I anxiously looked at the change list, I gasped. I can't believe it. This change list is three pages long too and on legal-size paper. I am sad. I am bewildered that I agreed to do this. I'm gritting my teeth. That's bad. Many of these changes definitely change the context of what was really said.

Oh well, when I'm wearing a bright orange suit and shackled at the ankles, I'll have an awful lot of explaining to do. My integrity has gone down the drain. Now I am agreeing to do what I consider criminal acts out of fear of retribution from Vincent Pagglione and his cronies. I have fear, also, of not knowing who to turn to for advice. This is a nightmare. My life is spiraling out of control.

Thank goodness Allison didn't know what else was on Pagglione's mind.

CHAPTER 23

The September 16th Grand Jury session was somewhat routine. When I left the courthouse that evening, I was cautious. I got in my car quicker than usual. I feel a sense of danger. For the life of me, I don't know if my mind is playing tricks on me or if I am completely going whacko.

Friday morning, around 10:30, mother called. She was ecstatic.

"Allison, guess what?"

"What? Is it good news?"

"Yes. Your dad and I are going to submit our papers in the spring of next year to serve a mission."

"Oh, mother, that is wonderful."

"Allie, the Lord has been good to us. We have been blessed to have each other and you kids. You know, we have always wanted to go on a mission, but we felt it was better to wait until you kids were raised. We both are in good health, and we feel strongly that this is a good time to serve the Lord."

"One thing for certain, mother, you and daddy will be great missionaries. I'm so happy for you. I'm also proud to be your daughter. You have served the Lord in so many generous ways, and you have been a great example to me all of my life."

"Oh, Allie, those words have made my day. Thank you, honey.

By the way Lydia is anxious for you to see Timothy. I can't wait for us to be together in Park City for Thanksgiving."

"I can't wait myself. It will be so much fun. I'm glad Timothy is healthy."

"It is such a blessing. Well, Allie, I'll talk to you soon. I love you so much."

"I love you mother. Bye-Bye."

Mother and daddy are so precious. They have worked so hard all their lives. They will be outstanding missionaries.

Tuesday rolled around, and I am praying that I can hold up under the pressure of this Grand Jury case. Pagglione appeared in the courtroom beaming. He is extremely pleased with himself, as usual. The Grand Jurors asked to recall a few witnesses to question them again.

Rosie is exuberant too. The longer we meet in these sessions, the more questions she asks of the witnesses. Some of her questions are totally idiotic.

At the end of the session Pagglione discussed with the Grand Jury members the fact that they more than likely would be completing the testimony before Thanksgiving. I feel relief. Music to my ears.

On the following Thursday, the videographers returned to testify for the last time. Oh my gosh, John Barker's face tells it all. He looks so disgusted. He has been through a lot. He is a tough guy.

John Barker is called to the witness stand first to testify, and it is an enjoyable experience for me. He won't give Pagglione an inch. He stands his ground and is definitely more intelligent than most of the other witnesses that have testified thus far. What a gutsy guy he is. I really admire his tenacity.

Sam Lucas, on the other hand, when he is testifying, seems afraid of his own shadow and chooses his words very carefully. He looks at the Grand Jurors with fear in his eyes. He has guilt written all over his face. Bless his heart.

It is amazing how easily the District Attorneys can intimidate some of these people. They are so afraid that their voices shake. They look so startled and miserable while they are testifying.

I know without a shadow of a doubt that Pagglione has intimidated me deliberately, but my attitude is changing, thanks to prayer, and I have decided to try to become more self-assured and confident. I am fed up with this whole situation. I do feel devastated, because I haven't asserted myself. I know in my heart that Pagglione is out to get me. I'm also beginning to realize that if I'm going to survive this ordeal I will have to fight every inch of the way to save myself.

The Grand Jury recessed for the evening, and Pagglione told the Grand Jurors they would meet again on September 28th and to take a break on September 30th, and then sometime in October or November they would more than likely have the case wrapped up.

Rosie is laughing. I have done a good job of avoiding her. She annoyed me from the beginning of this case by what she said, and using the word "friend" has constantly worried me. She is stupid but could possibly be dangerous.

Tuesday, September 28th, the Grand Jury session, again, was routine. My mood is beginning to improve with the knowledge that we are coming to a conclusion.

On Wednesday morning I got a call from Sarah. She was on her way to New York City the next day, and she was so excited.

"Sarah, you sound so happy."

"I wish you were going with me, Allie."

I was sincere when I told her, "I would give anything if I were free enough so that I could be with you to celebrate. Let the spotlight shine on you, Sarah."

"You are great, Allie."

I laughed. "I mean it Sarah. You deserve to be in the spotlight."

"Thank you, Allie.

I mailed 25 of my paintings to the Art Gallery in New York City. All of the artists will be displaying their art work at the Waldorf. I will be staying there as well."

"Wow, what a wonderful opportunity for you."

"Yes, and maybe I will be lucky enough to sell some of my paintings. Wouldn't that be rewarding?"

"Rewarding isn't the word for it. It's what you have worked for all of your life. You were doodling when you were five-years-old. I did not realize that you were showing 25 paintings. Wow, you have really been busy."

"Yes, I have."

"Well, Sarah, have a safe trip and be sure and call me over the weekend. You know, I am feeling a little jealous right now. I also feel guilty that I can't travel with you to hear all the accolades that you will be receiving."

"You nut. I love you Allie, and I will call you from the Waldorf."

"Okay. I love you, too." Good luck, Sarah. Bye-bye."

I put on my silk lounging robe, made a cup of herbal tea, and sat on my deck trying to sort together my own life. I am bound and determined, after this case is completed, to find out who is involved in this conspiracy, and then I will be able to make the right contacts and tell them in detail about the criminal activities that have taken place in these Grand Jury sessions.

On the very morning that Allison was contemplating what action she was going to take against Pagglione and his cronies, Vincent Pagglione was sitting with Judge Zacharelli behind closed doors in his chambers. Chief Judge Nicholas Zacharelli was spouting off with statements like, "That Allison Smith is such a beautiful young woman. I know that she is a Mormon. You know, I'm not completely certain that we made the right decision in having her be the Court Reporter for this case. She is very religious. I know for a fact that she doesn't drink or smoke. Let's face it, Vinny, she is a goody two shoes." The Judge leaned back in his high back leather chair. His face was red and puffed up as he bellowed out with his obnoxious laughter. He was blowing smoke through his nose from a Camel cigarette held by a slender ivory cigarette holder. The Rules, of course, don't apply to Chief Judge Zacharelli, the No Smoking Rules in the courthouse, anyway.

Pagglione laughed so hard he could hardly speak clearly to voice his opinion about Allison. "You know what I think, Nick?" The Judge is on a first-name basis with Pagglione.

"No. What?"

"You are right. Maybe we didn't make the right decision. Allison Smith is a little sneak. I am convinced by observing her all of these months that she won't keep her mouth shut. I have been pondering this over in my mind, and I have decided that you can't trust her to be one of us, a team player, if you will."

"Well, Vinny, if worse gets to worse, I'll leave it up to you to make the right decisions. You know what you may have to do, but don't make any mistakes, and I mean it."

"Everything has gone smoothly so far, Nick, and you know you can trust me."

"You realize I won't back you up, Vinny, if something goes wrong. I want to be perfectly clear about that right now."

"Yeah, I know. Well, I better be going, Nick. Hey, how about a golf game on Saturday?"

"I'd love to, Vinny. Why not." The Judge loved to play golf with Pagglione. Both of them were highly competitive.

"I will meet you out at the Country Club, Nick, say seven o'clock Saturday morning?"

"Sure thing. Keep your cool, Vinny, and everything will be fine."

"I will. Thanks, Nick. See you Saturday."

When Pagglione left the Judge's chamber, he felt stressed out and worried. He knew for sure that he could not trust Allison Smith, and he knew for sure that the Judge would look the other way and would never be in his corner if he fouled up. He also wasn't exactly sure of what steps to take to make certain that Allison was silenced. He knew, without a shadow of a doubt, he would be forced to use Dino in the end.

CHAPTER 24

At the Thursday night Grand Jury session everything went pretty much routinely until the break. I glanced over at Rosie and Vincent. I couldn't help but notice that they were overly-friendly. They are talking and laughing like they know each other. It appears strange to me.

At the end of the session Pagglione outlined the schedule for the Grand Jurors in October. "We will recall the witnesses you have requested to be heard again, and then at the end of on October, if all goes as planned, we will be presenting an indictment to you.

I need to, again, remind you of the importance of having a quorum present. Everyone should definitely be in attendance that evening. You will be voting on whether or not to go ahead with an indictment of Rita Clark, and John Barker and Sam Lucas, the videographers."

I am pretty good about predicting the outcome of a case but not in this case. I am plagued with confusion. I don't seem to be certain of anything anymore. The three-some have turned this trivial case into something much more serious. If they have convinced the jurors that this is a horrendous crime, Rita Clark, John Barker, and Sam Lucas will be indicted. In my opinion, that will be a travesty. An indictment of these good people is inconceivable, but I'm not able to read into my crystal ball on this one.

Vincent, in the meantime, is planning his strategy. He arranged with a friend of his, a close friend who owed him a favor, to go pick up Dino's Maserati and leave him an old Ford

Bronco. Pagglione wanted to make sure that Dino is in no way conspicuous when he visits the courthouse to survey the layout of the building.

Dino's orders are that he is to kill Allison on the last evening that the Grand Jurors meet to vote.

Pagglione called Dino on the phone. "Dino, how goes it?"

"Great. I have been hiking in the woods today. This isn't a bad lifestyle up here, you know it?"

If the truth be known, Dino is anxious to get back home. He lives in a mansion on the Isle of Capri in Italy, on top a hill overlooking the Mediterranean. He was born there, and his family are treated like royalty. They own a lot of real estate on Capri and also across the water in Naples.

Pagglione spoke sharply. "Well, hang tight, Dino. I am convinced that this little goody two shoes will have to be shut up once and for all. We all realize now that we can't trust her."

Dino was hoping that Pagglione would see it that way. He was elated and mumbled, One million dollars is already burning a hole in my pocket. "Well, boss, that's what I am here for."

Do you have everything you need?"

"I am a pro, remember?"

"Yeah, I know, Dino, but there can't be any slip-ups under any circumstances. Do you understand me?"

"I am not known to fail, boss. It will be clean as a whistle, and I will be out of here on the next plane headed for Italy." All

Dino could see was dollar signs. He is one of the highest paid hit men in the business, and he loves his status as well as the recognition he gets among his peers. He is proud of who he is and how superior he is. As a matter of fact, he has killed some very important people; for instance, well-known politicians and celebrities. Dino has said on many occasions, "This job will be a piece of cake."

Pagglione tried to act calm, but he was a nervous wreck. "I know I can count on you, Dino, to pull it off. Your money will be wired to you from a bank in Switzerland. A complete map will be given to you of the courthouse grounds as well as the interior of the building. Minute details will be mapped out for you. When my friend delivers the Bronco to you, he will give you a packet of instructions. I will be communicating with you by my private cell phone. I want you to destroy your phone before you leave for Italy. Do you understand?"

"Yes, boss. What do you think I am, an idiot or something? Hey, when this is all over with, we want you to come over for a celebration, Vinny. What do you say?"

"I'd love it. Keep the champagne on ice for me. I won't plan to come for six months or more, but I will be there. Do you mind if I bring my latest girlfriend along?"

"Hell, no. The more the merrier." Pagglione is dating a tall buxom blond who is somewhat of a klutz in the way of brains, but he likes those kind of girls, probably because he lacks common sense himself. He is riding high. He is pretty sure of himself nowadays.

Vincent Pagglione is strategizing the hit from all angles. He told himself: One thing I better do, just so there won't be any problems with McCallister or Summers, I need to bring them in on my plan. He called for a meeting on a Friday afternoon, and McCallister and Summers came running, as usual. Anytime Vinny said, "I need you guys in here," they jumped.

Vincent thought McCallister and Summers were sheep. He laughed to himself. The reason I chose them to work with me on this case is because I knew they would follow me, no matter what. Neither of them are smart enough to think for themselves. They are in my corner. That's all I care. They know I'm a win-win type of guy. They are so impressed by my expertise at running things. Who wouldn't be? Of course, if worse comes to worse, I'll save my own skin. That's the way the world operates.

Pagglione told his secretary that he did not want any calls to come through for the next two hours when McCallister and Summers arrived. They greeted each other in their usual friendly manner. It is a sickening sight to behold when they all get together. McCallister and Summers are nauseatingly obsequious towards Pagglione. They are at the height of their glory, and they thought they could do no wrong. It was going just the way they wanted it to go. All of them were in high spirits, but underneath they were stressed out to the max about the outcome.

They felt like they had the Grand Jurors in the palm of their hands, and McCallister was looking for Pagglione to be a Senator one day, and he definitely had ambitions of his own. He was bound and determined to tag along. Summers also thought she could fit into politics quite nicely, and Pagglione would pave the way for her as well. So they both played the game to the hilt. They would wallow in the mud, if necessary, to get ahead.

Pagglione began talking fast, but he was trying to keep cool. He had black circles under his eyes from lack of sleep. He is beginning to feel a lot of pressure.

"Look, guys, this Allison Smith is not who I thought she was, easy prey, if you know what I mean." Pagglione didn't really want to come out and admit he'd made a big mistake in thinking Allison could be trusted. "I'm certain now she can't be trusted. She comes off too innocent for me, and remember this and don't forget it, we will all go down the drain if she opens her big mouth. My feeling is, the most likely time she will blow the whistle is when the indictments come down, and we will feel like running for cover. We can't take the chance, can we now?" Pagglione is trying to feel them out as to how far they would really go and if they were with him all the way. He wanted assurance to see just how much power he had over them.

McCallister shook his head. "Whatever we have to do, Vinny. You know we will support you all the way."

Summers then chimed in, "It would be a disaster for all of us. What are you proposing, Vinny?"

Pagglione gave Summers a wink and a phony smile. He is beginning to feel more assured of their loyalty to him. This he demanded of all his subordinates, their complete and unwavering obedience. This feeling of power sustained him in his hours of weakness.

He spoke boldly now and with a strong conviction as he revealed his plans, knowing now that they were all in this together. They would all stick together like glue and come out on top. He was convinced of that as he looked into their faces, and he was thrilled at the thought of his magnificent political future.

"Well, this is the last resort, guys, but we have no choice. I have hired a hit man, and he is lined up to knock Allison off the evening that we present the indictments."

McCallister didn't hesitate on his next comment. "Whatever has to be done. It's our necks or hers."

Even Pagglione was surprised at their reactions. He thought he might meet with some adversity, but it was all falling into his hands just the way he wanted it to. He was proud of himself and them. He was very careful who he selected to be on his team in this case, and there was no doubt in his mind that he had made the right choices. They would play the game exactly as he had planned it, and they would go along with him right up to the end without any trouble. Of course, they all had a lot to lose and knew it. None of them were willing to take a chance on losing their careers. They all intended to climb the ladder with Pagglione.

McCallister asked in a very serious tone of voice, "What's the next step, Vinny?" He realized there was no backing out.

Vincent Pagglione spoke in an angry tone. "I feel Allison Smith is cocky and self-assured, and the more I am around her, the more I detest her. "Well, without going into all the details, we have got our hit man. He's a pro. It will cost us a million bucks, but that has been taken care of. The money will be laundered through a Swiss Bank. So there will never be a possibility of tracing it. I wanted to make sure that you would give me the go ahead."

McCallister came alive and said: "You have got it. Just make sure that nothing goes wrong, Vinny." Summers nodded in agreement, but her worn-out face told another story.

Pagglione continued: "Like I said, he's a top-notch pro. He has been hired by the best. For one million bucks, he ought to be worth his salt at that price. There is no problem with him whatsoever." McCallister and Summers were satisfied.

McCallister wanted to change the subject, always with himself in mind. "Of course, I am with you all the way if you decide to run for Senator, Vinny. I think you would make a wonderful Senator." He beamed as he assured Pagglione of his support.

Pagglione beamed as well. "Thanks. I am seriously thinking about it. It's in my blood, politics, and I think I could do a lot of good for the people here in the State of Colorado. I will be committed to being honest, and I feel I would do an excellent job."

Summers was delighted. "You're our man, Vinny. Anything I can do for you, just holler. You have got the right stuff. You can win, and we'll be right there to support you all the way."

Pagglione was eating this stuff up. He loved to be admired. He was in his glory that Friday afternoon, just thinking about his future. Allison Smith was just a number as far as he was concerned and nothing, no nothing would get in his way. His thoughts were, of late, that he was on his way to the top, maybe even running for the presidency.

While Pagglione, McCallister, and Summers were planning to have a hit man murder Allison, she was beginning to look ahead.

I am feeling so much better. I think I will shop this weekend. There is a big sale at Gart Brothers downtown Denver. I want to buy myself a new ski outfit for the family Park City trip, and I also want to buy a special gift for Lydia and the new baby as well as some gifts for my nieces and nephews. I want to be generous to my family. I will send them money as well.

I found a sea blue metallic ski outfit at Gart's, top of the line brand, and I splurged and bought all matching accessories. The sales clerk told me I looked gorgeous in the ski outfit. My spirits are elevating. For the first time in a long time, I feel a tinge of optimism.

On Sunday, Sarah called from New York City. "Allie, hi." She sounds overwhelmed with excitement.

"Is this Ms. Sarah Taylor, artist extraordinaire?"

"Allie, don't tease me."

"What's happening?"

"Well, you won't believe it."

"Try me."

"I am so excited. I sold seven of my paintings."

"Why am I not surprised?"

"You know the one I did of the Pine View Dam and the mountains in the background up in Ogden Canyon?"

"Yes."

"That painting sold for $25,000."

"That is wonderful. You are a celebrity."

"Well, I will tell you one thing, Allie. The work and pain of it all has been worth it. I was beginning to doubt myself, but things are coming together for me."

"You better believe it, Sarah, and it couldn't happen to somebody more deserving than you."

"Allie, you would love New York City. It is the most exciting place in the world. You don't have to go to the theater to be entertained. You can sit on a bench in Central Park and be thoroughly mesmerized by the people that you see, all varieties. The heartbeat of the city is hard to explain. When they say New York City has it all, there is truth in that statement. It's unbelievable. I feel like I'm on another planet. Seriously, Allie. I'm not kidding."

"You are making me jealous, you know it."

"Well, Allie, I hate to make you jealous, but guess where I am invited to go tomorrow?"

"New York City is a place I've always wanted to visit. The thought of Broadway, the theater. It gives me goose bumps. Anyway, where are you going tomorrow?"

"Allie, I am afraid to tell you. You won't be mad at me, will you?"

I paused before I spoke. "Yes."

Sarah laughed. "The Statue of Liberty."

I am all choked up. "Tell her I love her, and I'll visit her. She is on my bucket list. I promise. You know, Sarah, the French people are so generous. They presented our country with this magnificent gift that represents the best in all of us. She stands in the harbor, so proudly, for so many years."

"Allie, you have got to get out from under all that work, all those deadlines. It's beginning to make me, your best friend, crazy. Please, come with me to New York City on my next exhibition."

"I promise you one thing, Sarah. I will. I will do just that."

"Got to go, Allie. I will call you when I get back to Ogden. I am going up to the cabin for a week when I get home."

"Okay. Sarah, I knew you would knock them dead."

"Thank you for your love and support. I appreciate it more than you can imagine. Love you, Allie."

"Love you too, Sarah."

I am so thrilled for Sarah's success. I still can't help feeling lonely inside right this moment. She is right. I am overworking and missing out on too much. I also know that self-pity isn't going to do me any good. Sometimes I think about Todd and what my life would have been like. I loved him so much. He was my world. Still, I'm not going to lose hope.

My first priority, after this case is over, is to try to find someone who honors his priesthood. I want to be married in the temple. I want to have an eternal family. I don't like to discuss it with mother and daddy or anyone for that matter. I need to face reality and move on. It's difficult to do sometimes. Praying has helped a lot. I never would have survived without knowing that my Heavenly Father and Savior love me and will protect me.

CHAPTER 25

I am going to jog for at least an hour to get the cobwebs out of my head. The day is so beautiful, just a slight breeze. The sun shining brightly gives me a feeling of euphoria. It won't be long now and I will be able to feel freedom. When I get more time, I want to concentrate on doing something worthwhile, such as spend more time with my family.

I hate to go indoors and begin working. The minute I stepped into the house, the phone rang. It's mother. Thank goodness. The sound of Vinny's voice puts me in a panic. I resent him and his cronies to the max.

"Hi sweetheart. I am glad I caught you home. How are you doing?"

"Hi mother. I'm fine." I cannot burden mother with all my troubles.

"Well, I just wanted to tell you that we are looking forward to having a wonderful get-together in Park City at Thanksgiving. I can't wait to see you. I love you and miss you so much."

"I can't wait to be with all the family. I love you and miss you."

"Honey, my other line is ringing. I need to go now."

"Take care. Give everyone my love." I wish I could pour my heart out to mother and daddy but why worry them. Crying all the time certainly isn't going to get me anywhere. Besides, adversity can be the beginning of building a better me. President

Hinkley always tells us to do the best that we can. I think about that, especially lately.

Back to work.

Pagglione is becoming extremely nervous. His confident demeanor is beginning to change. His face has broken out in a red rash, and he is frantic about that; that he would appear less than perfect.

He placed a call to Dino. As he spoke, he is frowning and his tone of voice is demanding.

"Dino."

"Yeah, boss."

"You need to listen to me carefully. I want you to dress like a professional. Get rid of the black clothing and get your hair cut. Spend some time in the courthouse for the next couple of weeks. Scour the building. Get to know every nook and cranny so that you can get in and out of the courthouse quickly."

"Hey, Vinny, you sound like a bag of nerves." Pagglione was beginning to detest Dino's nonchalant ways. They were complete opposites, but he needed him badly.

"Well, you could say I don't want anybody to foul up the plan, if you know what I mean." Pagglione wasn't about to admit to Dino that he was a bag of nerves.

"What do you think I am, Vinny? You are not dealing with a rooky here. I have never messed up before, and I don't intend to now. Keep your cool." Dino didn't want to say anything to Vinny, but he was anxious to get back to the Isle of Capri and relax for a couple of months. He was feeling isolated and needed to be with his own kind. He had already calculated his debt level and the million bucks was looking mighty good. He was going over and over his next purchases, figuring out every last dime and how he would spend it. A fancy luxury boat was first on his list. He needed the million bucks desperately. A large portion of the money would go to save him from bankruptcy.

Pagglione is beginning to lose his temper with Dino, and he shouted into the phone. "It looks like we are beginning to wrap things up. Our target date is October 14th. What I have planned is for you to enter the courthouse when I give you the go sign."

"Where will you be, Boss?"

"That night we will present the indictments. We have convinced the Grand Jurors, no doubt, of the guilt of Rita Clark and the videographers, and when the jury comes back with the indictments, we will meet the media outside at the entrance of the courthouse. The media will be surrounding the front portion of the courthouse, sticking cameras in our faces, wanting to get the latest news about Rita Clark."

I'm more than confident that Rita Clark and the videographers will be indicted. After all, I have covered every aspect of the case. I have been meticulous.

"When the coast is clear and everybody is out in the front of the courthouse, I will give you the go signal. Everyone will be so distracted with the media frenzy that you can then get into the building by the back entrance without ever being seen by anyone. You can use the stairwell to get to the 4th floor."

"Won't someone be in the building, boss, a janitor, maybe?"

"No. I will make sure that no one is in the building, Dino, except you and the Court Reporter. I want to be assured nothing goes wrong. I mean nothing. Do you understand?"

"Yeah, boss. I will do everything you say. Don't worry about anything. You can count on me. You know that."

"This gal is a bit smarter than the average. So you have got to be on your toes."

"Lighten up, boss." Dino wanted to change the subject. Pagglione is driving him crazy with that excitable tone of voice.

"Hey, we will be calling you Senator before long, boss."

Pagglione grinned. "It's true. Thanks."

I am bound to rise to the top. No doubt about it. I feel confident about being on the right road, headed to Washington D.C. I certainly don't want any stupid Court Reporter ruining my plans.

"I hear you loud and clear, boss."

"Okay, Dino, you got it? I want you to know that courthouse by the back of your hand and pay attention to every detail. Above all, be discrete. Try to be as invisible as you can be."

Pagglione hated incompetence and thought: I much prefer to do everything myself. In actuality, I don't trust anyone else. If I want it done right, I have to do it myself. I know that I can do most everything better than most people. Sometimes it irritates me to death to have to delegate, even the smallest jobs.

"I will be talking to you next Sunday, Dino, and we will go over everything in detail. Do you understand?"

"Got it, boss." The conversation ended on that note.

Pagglione muttered to himself: Dino aggravates the hell out of me. Still, I'm satisfied at how things are going so far. Once Allison Smith is out of the picture, all of us will breathe easier. No one can get in the way of my ambitions. No, not anyone.

CHAPTER 26

Monday morning Chief Judge Zacharelli sat in his Chambers waiting for Pagglione. He was deep in thought. Where is he? He is never late. I don't know why but I'm becoming increasingly impatient with him. Down deep I have always despised the guy. He is too precise for me and thinks too much of himself. I have to go along with the situation as it is. That's life in a nut shell.

Pagglione entered the Judge's chambers with a grin on his face. "Good morning, Nick."

"Good morning, Vinny." Judge Zacharelli slipped a cigarette into his ivory cigarette holder and with his silver cigarette lighter lit up, and he blew smoke out of his nose with a great feeling of satisfaction.

Pagglione sat there thinking: The Judge is so amusing. He's such a clown.

"Vinny, I'll be back in a minute. You know how it is. Nature calls."

Pagglione looked around the Judge's chambers in disgust. He could hardly bear to look at the papers piled high. Such disorganization. Nick is the slob of all slobs. How can he find anything in this mess? We are opposites. It is amazing how we get along at all. There is not much I actually like about him.

I have to be cautious and deal with him as tactfully as possible. It won't be for much longer, hopefully. Whether I like it or not, I need Nick for political reasons. The Judge is a professional politician, a real slap-on-the-back kind of guy. I cannot forget that down the road Nick will be a real asset to me come election time. Flatter the old goat. Stay on his good side under any circumstances.

The Judge returned and slapped Vinny on the back. "Your Honor, how are you today?"

"Well, Vinny, it is Monday, isn't it? How are any of us on a Monday? I didn't like the fact that you skunked me at golf on Saturday." The Judge burst out laughing. His laughter is contagious. When he laughs, it is so loud that everyone within an earshot distance can hear him. Vinny joined right in on the laughter.

Craziest thing, Vinny thought: Nick is of the opinion that everyone thinks the world of him when the opposite is actually true. Most people, behind his back, make fun of him. He is the butt of most of the jokes going around the courthouse.

Vinny spoke to the Judge in a serious tone. "You know, Nick, I don't think we have any choice but to go ahead with our plans."

The Judge's face soured. "I was hoping, Vinny, that you wouldn't have to resort to anything too drastic, not murder, but I also realize it might be the only way to shut the girl up." The Judge and Pagglione grinned.

"Nick, I don't trust her. It is difficult to figure out what she is thinking. She is so standoffish lately. I feel certain that she will open her mouth eventually. So far, from what I can see, she is afraid, but later on down the road when she thinks about it, I know she won't keep her mouth shut."

The Judge shifted uncomfortably in his leather chair. "When Allison came in and talked to me, I thought the same thing. One thing for sure, she is a beauty, don't you think?"

"Yeah, Nick, but she is too self-righteous for me." Zacharelli burst out laughing. Pagglione faked a laugh, thinking: There is nothing the Judge likes better than vulgarity. Old Zacharelli is getting pretty forgetful. He has repeated himself time and time again about Allison being a goody two shoe type of girl. His jokes are getting old, especially the third time around. They are not even funny. Geez, he doesn't even remember what he said the day before yesterday. Senility is setting in, or worse yet Alzheimer's. I'd bet my life on it. Although, sometimes he is amusing in an odd sort of way.

If it be known, Zacharelli is not the nice guy he wants everyone to think he is. Still, I have to be careful and say the right things. I have to make sure the Judge feels that we are on the same page and make him think that we are the best of friends.

"You know, Nick, Allison Smith, is so uptight. She reminds me of my mother." Down deep Pagglione hated women.

"Well, Vinny, do what you have got to do, but don't bother me with the details." Zacharelli was not one bit interested in being implicated. He said to himself: I have the goods on Vinny. There is no way he can drag me into any wrongdoing if something goes awry. He's not as squeaky-clean as he tries to pretend he is. His past is full of many questionable dealings. He is and can be dangerous because of his connections. I'm clear. I'm in an excellent position to just sit back and make out like all is well, and I'll damn well protect myself if things get sticky-wicked.

I'm anxious to get rid of Vinny. I need to dictate an Order that had been sitting on my desk too long. I'm a procrastinator, but so what. I'm feeling stress with this Grand Jury problem.

The Judge blurted out, "Be careful, Vinny. You hear me." Well, I have to sound like I care. I don't give a damn about Pagglione, McCallister, Morgan Summers, or Allison Smith. They are all just pawns in the whole scheme of things. At this point all I want is to rid myself of the whole situation. It definitely is getting a bit too close to home for me.

Pagglione felt the Judge's demeanor change, and he knew that it was time to get up and leave. "I'll keep you up to date on what's going on, Nick."

"Yes, Vinny. You do that. Talk to you later. Hey, we need a rematch. Let's get together more often for some golf. What do you say?"

"I agree Nick. See you soon."

Pagglione, struggling to think positive, thought: I felt like I was suffocating in Nick's chambers. I also feel a knot in my stomach. Everything must go down as planned.

Even Dino worries me. I fear he will turn into a bumbling idiot and screw up the whole works. He is a pro, but sometimes he appears so awkward.

I feel like I definitely need a change of pace. Hawaii sounds good right at this very moment. Beach. Palm Trees.

Women. He grumbled: It will be over soon. I'll make up for all of this work and worry by taking time off. I'll block my calendar off for a month when the time is right.

The week passed without incident, and on the 12th day of October, the Grand Jury case was finally winding down.

After this evening, we will have only one more session of Grand Jury. This case is finally almost concluded. Thank goodness. I am getting more rest, and I don't feel as depressed, even though I still feel unusual fatigue at times, but not too bad.

Pagglione spoke to the Grand Jurors:

"Members of the Grand Jury, you will be receiving the indictments for deliberation on Thursday of this week. You need to be sure that you are in attendance. It is mandatory that we have a quorum present so that you can vote.

Also, I need to tell you ahead of time that there will be a media frenzy outside of the courthouse that evening. They will be hounding me for more details on the results of the Grand Jury case."

I felt an unusual calmness come over me as we began the session, but I couldn't help thinking about how I have survived this whole ordeal. Vincent has been so wicked throughout this case.

He is in rare form tonight. Man alive, he loves to hear himself speak. He is articulate, but anyone knowing the man like I do can see right through him without too much trouble.

For some reason the Grand Jurors seem completely mesmerized with this case and with Vincent Pagglione. I have to hand it to him, because he has definitely done a good job of convincing the Jurors that Rita Clark and the videographers are criminals who have committed heinous crimes.

I can hardly focus on writing the words down. My mind is somewhere else. I know it will just be a matter of time that I will be able to discover who I can trust. As soon as I do, I am going to tell the truth, even if it means I'm implicated. It is important that the public knows what has transpired in this case. They need to know all about the manipulation of the Grand Jurors; the criticism by Vincent of Rita Clark and her attorney off the record; the corruptness of going off the record while talking to the Jurors, and I have tremendous guilt that I followed the orders of Vincent Pagglione and changed the words on the original transcripts.

Vincent has tried in every way possible to get indictments of Rita Clark and the videographers. He has spoken about them as if they are professional criminals.

As for myself, I am sick and tired of being afraid to come forward. Vincent Pagglione, if I have anything to do with this, you are not going to get off scot-free. I feel like I have been caught in a web of deceit and lies.

Pagglione brought one witness back for just a few short questions. One of the Grand Jurors needed to clarify something through Raymond Mitchell's testimony. That was the last testimony to be heard by the Grand Jurors, and the case was laid to rest.

It is over. I am elated.

CHAPTER 27

On the following Thursday, while driving to the courthouse, I was thinking: I feel a tinge of joy, but still I'm apprehensive. This is the final session of the case. No matter what, I am not going to give up on my intentions. I'm fearful for my own life, but I have the comfort of the Lord, and I know he wants me to be true to myself. Honestly is always the best policy.

I am so glad I have kept a detailed journal regarding everything that has transpired. It can be used as evidence in the future. I know when I tell everything, Vincent and his cronies will want to retaliate and it won't be pretty, but under no circumstances am I going to let that stop me. The fear is coming from not knowing exactly what the outcome will be.

My last entry that I wrote in my journal says, "I fear that Vincent Pagglione and his cronies are going to try to kill me to keep me from telling the truth." I hope I live long enough to be able to say that I fought back and then remind myself that I must go forward.

Dino spent all week cruising the halls of the courthouse, flitting here and there and trying to blend in. He sat in on a personal injury case and in trying not to look suspicious, he took breaks when the Jury did.

Pagglione kept thinking about Dino: I'm so disgusted with him. I know that he will be careful. He keeps harping on the fact that he is a professional, a real pro. From his reputation, I feel assured that he is.

Pagglione was moody the whole day. By evening he was highly irritated. When he walked into the courtroom and stood and watched Allison as she set up her equipment, he said to himself: I hate that woman. I don't like her personality. She is trouble. I'm willing to go to any length to get rid of trouble. No one will stand in my way.

After I set up my equipment, I sat down and actually feel a sense of rejuvenation. I think even my sense of humor is returning. Watching Pagglione, McCallister, and Morgan Summers parade down the aisle to greet the Grand Jurors is hilarious. They are so caught up in the moment. Although my thoughts are flip-flopping, I cannot help but smile to myself. Then I said under my breath: Life is a comedy of errors. It is almost over. Keep your composure.

Pagglione is dressed like he is going to attend a coronation. I can't believe he is for real. What's with the beige silk suit, silk tie, and, wow, leather Italian shoes. We must not forget, this is his big night. He is going to get his mug before the cameras. He is over-dressed for the occasion, and over-confident, as usual, but, let's face it, it has all the makings of a comical sitcom if it wasn't so pitiful.

McCallister actually looks better than usual. His tie looks new. It is hanging neat as a pin which is so unlike his usual manner of dress and the right color. His suit and shirt have been meticulously selected. It certainly is an improvement. I'm sure that Vincent had a hand in his new look.

Morgan Summers is wearing some make-up, and she has a reasonably good looking suit on. Admittedly, there is not much Morgan Summers can do to improve her appearance. She is a hopeless person, but no dummy, just a follower to the max, someone who will dance to anybody's tune if it looks like there is something in it for her.

Pagglione is standing before the podium in all his glory and begins to speak directly to the Grand Jurors. He glances over at me.

"On the record."' I begin to write. Pagglione is speaking, attempting to be sincere. "Well, it's been a long haul, but Members of the Grand Jury we are finally at the finish line. I would like to welcome you this evening and thank all of you for coming. I also would like to thank all of you for your hard work on this case. It can be very difficult at times, and we appreciate your service. We needed your cooperation in every way, and that is exactly what we got. In fact, you are the best and most attentive group that we have ever had."

I could not help but laugh inside, because he tells every group of Grand Jurors the same thing. If they only knew the real Vincent Pagglione. His has no moral fiber.

Then Pagglione went on to present the indictments. He carried on for at least another 45 minutes, and then he excused the Grand Jurors, and told them to take a brief break in the jury room but not to leave the jury room for any reason; that refreshments would be brought in for them.

The Grand Jurors then rose and proceeded out of the courtroom, single file, to begin their deliberations. As soon as the Grand Jurors were gone, Pagglione turned to McCallister and Summers and said: "I'll bet that they will be back with indictments within the hour." He is always so sure of himself. Of course, everyone agreed with him. How could they not. They were all looking for greener pastures.

I always knew that McCallister and Summers were hanging on Pagglione's coattails, because I overheard a great deal of their conversations.

Pagglione nervously checked his watch carefully as time passed.

I muttered: I'm nervous, but I do not want to show it.

In the meantime, the media was gathering outside. They had set up all the equipment necessary. There were five television stations ready to go, all anxious to get the final results on Rita Clark and the videographers; all waiting to spring on the District Attorneys as they came out of the courthouse.

It was getting around nine o'clock. Pagglione paced back and forth. He mumbled to himself: I'm worried and wondering what the Grand Jurors are up to.

Rosie was selected to be the forewoman of the Grand Jury. She is delighted. She was hoping that the members would select her.

Everything seemed to be working out just as Pagglione had planned. He kept thinking that once Allison is out of the picture, Rosie, at my suggestion, will stay six more months working at the library in Arvada, leaving nothing to suspicion, and then she could turn in her resignation. By then, with a job well done, she could return to her home in Italy, the Isle of Capri.

Rosie and Dino are cousins. They work together on many jobs that require both of them. They have a great working relationship.

Rosie is in her element as forewoman of the Grand Jury. She begins to speak. "These crimes should not go unnoticed. We are obligated to return indictments on all three, Rita Clark, John Barker, and Sam Lucas. In all sincerity, we need to send a strong message to Rita Clark and the videographers that they cannot take it upon themselves to stage a story. It is a horrendous crime."

At 8:15 p.m. pizza was delivered to the Grand Jurors in the jury room. They finished eating and they began their deliberations. After a very short deliberation, a vote was taken. Rosie beamed as she announced, "It is unanimous. Rita Clark and the videographers are indicted."

The mood was cordial among the Grand Jurors as to their decision. Rosie was relieved to receive an indictment so quickly.

She said, "I have enjoyed working with you. You are a great bunch of people. I wish you luck in the future. We have had a lot of laughs and joked around quite a bit. I'll miss seeing you."

The timing was perfect. Dino was a couple of miles away from the courthouse in the old Bronco. He turned up the volume on the radio and sang at the top of his lungs with the music as if he was on his way to a celebration instead of on his way to murder Allison Smith.

Dino is boisterous and, in most respects, crude. He is waiting impatiently for the big call from Vinny. Actually, as planned, there is supposed to be two calls.

At that moment the phone rang. Dino picked up his phone immediately and said to Pagglione, "Boss, is that you?"

Pagglione is furious. "Who do you think it would be, you idiot? I sure as hell hope you weren't expecting it to be somebody else."

Exasperated, Pagglione thought: I'm fit to be tied. My nerves are shot. I have to depend upon this numskull not to make a mistake. Dino is dumber than dumb. "Look, Dino, my friend, get yourself down to the courthouse now. Park where I told you to park and wait for my next call."

"Okay, boss." Dino smiles and shouts, Pagglione is a stuffed shirt. He thinks he's a big shot. Man, he has no street smarts whatsoever. I can't stand the guy. I'm looking forward to splitting.

Vincent Pagglione is told that the Grand Jurors have reached a decision. The bailiff is instructed by Pagglione to bring the Grand Jurors back to the courtroom. The Grand Jurors entered the courtroom one by one.

At this point Pagglione is looking frazzled. He mumbles: I will not reveal to anybody about how I'm feeling. McCallister and Summers are counting on me. They trust me and are comforted because of the fact that I never slip up. I never make a mistake. So they have no reason whatsoever to worry. Everything will go as planned, and I could possibly be going to Washington D.C. with them. They are as ambitious as I am. Although I doubt I would consider them for a position.

I sat in silence waiting to go on the record. Vincent is nodding at me to begin.

"Members of the Grand Jury, have you reached a decision in this case?" Rosie handed the document to Vincent. It is signed by the Grand Jurors. Pagglione's demeanor changed immediately. He is grinning from ear to ear as the indictments are read.

Rita Clark is indicted on 17 felony counts, and the videographers are indicted on two felonies each. Rita Clark slumped in her chair and grabbed hold of her attorney. Sinclair Bennett looks furious. John Barker and Sam Lucas shook their heads in disbelief.

I am flabbergasted. How in the world did they come up with 17 felonies for Rita Clark and two felonies each for John Barker and Sam Lucas? Pagglione, McCallister and Summers, without a doubt, have no conscience. They are undeniably wicked. I am sick to my stomach and feel hostility toward all of them.

Pagglione spoke: "Thank you, again, for your service. We appreciate your time and effort in doing your best and keeping an open mind."

I grimaced. What a joke.

"Please," Pagglione said, "After you gather up your belongings, leave by the private exit. I don't want you to be bothered by the news media or harassed in any way."

Before they were escorted out, Rosie asked when the next case would be beginning. Pagglione said: "We want to give you a rest. The next case will not be heard until after the first of the year."

Always thinking of himself first, I know for a fact that Pagglione is bound and determined to take as much time off as he can get.

"Members of the jury, you are now excused with our sincere thanks."

Rita Clark, Sinclair Bennett, and the videographers walked out of the courtroom. They look distraught. Sinclair Bennett looks like he could strangle someone if he got a chance. Apparently they have a limo waiting for them.

You could tell by the look on Pagglione's face that he was so glad to be rid of everyone. He grumbled: "They are all a bunch of fools." Behind their backs he made all kinds of wise cracks about all of them. Pagglione always looks at the worst in people. He is brutal.

At this point, Pagglione has other things on his mind. He is a bundle of nerves, worrying about Dino and his so-called expertise. He kept looking at his watch.

CHAPTER 28

I am so disgusted. Vinny railroaded these Grand Jurors into thinking this was the crime of the century. He broke all the Rules of the Grand Jury. I am now more than ever convinced that bringing this case before the Grand Jury has kept him in the limelight, and he deliberately planned all along to use this trivial case to push his political career forward and get as much press coverage as possible. That's exactly what has happened.

He thinks he has won. I am still determined to tell everything I know when I find the right person, someone I am positive I can trust and someone that will realize the seriousness of the situation; someone that will listen to me and help me bring all the people involved in these criminal activities to justice.

At the same time, I feel so alone and petrified.

Pagglione looked at his watch again. Without saying a word to Allison, Pagglione, McCallister, and Summers abruptly walked out of the courtroom, ready to take on the media, but first Pagglione had to make a call.

Dino was sitting in the old Bronco about a block from the courthouse. He is impatiently waiting to hear from Pagglione. Pagglione had gone to one of the private offices in the courthouse. He took his private phone out of the carrier and dialed Dino.

Dino was beginning to feel high anxiety. He was finishing his fifth cigarette when the call came in.

Pagglione was as nervous as Dino.

"Dino, everyone is out in the front of the courthouse with the media. They are waiting on me. Allison is alone in the courtroom. You can make your move now. No fouling up the works. Got it?"

Dino is annoyed with Pagglione, sick to death of his obnoxious personality. "You can count on me, boss." Dino thought: I'm not stupid enough at this point to start an argument or even disagree with Vinny. We have nothing in common, except business. We are as different as night and day.

Pagglione's last words were, "It is time. Go for it." Then, Pagglione, feeling every nerve in his body quiver, walked swiftly from the private office and exited the courthouse to face the crowd and the media. He is full of anxiety, but he knows as soon as it is over and done with he can relax and begin to enjoy life again.

Dino, dressed in black, walked to the private entrance at the back of the courthouse and entered. There is no one in sight, just as Pagglione had said, that the back entrance of the courthouse would be free of people.

Still on the side of precaution, Dino put on his gloves and waited until he got inside the courthouse to put on his dark glasses. He started to climb the back stairs to the 4th Floor. He moved as silent as a cat.

Okay, I said to myself. It is over. Pack up your equipment. Thinking about the last several months makes me feel angrier by the minute. I will get that wicked Vincent Pagglione sooner or later.

I have now got to turn my thoughts around and focus on the brighter side of life. Just think, I'll be with my family and Sarah at Thanksgiving. Still, I cannot help but have compassion for Rita Clark and the videographers.

Dino reached the 4th Floor and crept toward the entrance to the Clerk's Office which led into the Judge's Chambers. It was conveniently unlocked. He slipped into the Clerk's office and quickly walked into the Judge's chambers. Dino pulled out his handgun with a silencer on it. Then, without too much hesitation, he quietly opened the door to the courtroom, the Judge's entrance to the bench.

For a few seconds, which seemed like hours, he observed Allison standing there in plain sight. No time was wasted. He pointed the gun at the back of Allison's head and fired. Just as Dino fired the weapon, Allison bent down to unzip her computer bag. The bullet missed, glazed the side of her head and hit the opposite side of the courtroom wall. Dino could hear the bullet as it hit the wall, a strange cracking sound.

I screamed, "That was a gunshot. Someone is trying to kill me." At this point, I am in shock. A terrifying chill ran through my body. My thoughts came quickly: Run! Run! Get out of here. Don't waste time.

Dino was stunned. He had never missed on a first shot. In fact, he was trained by experts in Italy. He is known to be a sharp shooter; one of the best in the country.

I ran to the back of the courtroom. As I did, the man in black pulled the trigger again, trying to shoot me in the back. I was too quick for him, and he missed again. The bullet lodged into the wall at the back of the courtroom.

At that point, Dino panicked.

I ran through the double doors from the courtroom and hit the exit to the stairs. I kept a cool head and told myself to run for my life.

Dino had failed, and he knew it was too late to go after her. He had to save his own neck. So he ran down the back exit and walked to his Bronco. No one was in sight. It was pitch black outside. He felt confident that he had not been seen. He got in the Bronco and started up the engine. He was badly shaken.

He thought: Forget about Pagglione. Every man for himself. That was Dino's motto in life. He had his airline ticket booked from Denver to New York and from New York to Rome, Italy. He was always prepared in case something went wrong, but he had never failed in getting the job done. His heart was racing and all he could think of was to get on that plane and get out of the country.

He appeased himself by admitting that everybody, pro or not, had their down days, but he was very disappointed about not earning the million bucks. Dino drove the speed limit but was anxious to get to the airport. He kept replaying what went wrong and consoling himself by thinking: Well, nobody is perfect.

I thanked the Lord for protection and am so grateful that I am in good shape; good enough to escape from being murdered.

The killer is not going to come after me. I reached the main floor and ran out of the entrance of the courthouse screaming, "Someone tried to kill me. Someone tried to kill me."

Pagglione heard me screaming, and he turned white as a sheet. I ran right through the middle of the crowd, straight up to Pagglione. My frightened look startled everyone. The cameramen were so surprised. Their first impulse was to immediately turn their cameras away from Pagglione. They focused them directly on me. At that moment, I was being televised live, and because I was in such a state of shock I didn't even realize I was on television. One of the television news reporters excitedly asked me, ""Who in the devil are you?"

I was out of breath and tears streamed down my face as I spoke: "Someone tried to kill me. I am Allison Smith, the Court Reporter for the Grand Jury. I was packing up my equipment, and somebody came out of the Judge's chambers and shot at me but missed. He shot again and missed."

The crowd is in disbelief. I am sure they thought that I was some sort of a crazy person at first. With the cameras still focused on me from every direction, I collapsed into the arms of Bill Daniels from Channel 5.

Pagglione is so shaken he could hardly believe what he was hearing. Without a moment's hesitation he pulled himself together. He thought to himself. I know I have to put on the greatest show of my career. Act shocked. Be compassionate toward the dumb gal.

Pagglione leaned over Allison. "Someone call 911." He is bound and determined to play it safe. Save my own skin. Look like I can't believe what has happened.

McCallister and Summers took their cues from Pagglione. They were afraid, but they followed suit and fell into their roles in a professional manner. They knew what they had to do. Go along. Keep cool. Act concerned about Allison's well- being. They realized at that moment that they had to do whatever it took to save their own skin.

The ambulance arrived and on live television Allison was carried to the vehicle on a gurney, and with sirens screaming she was taken to the hospital. The crowd was numb with terror, but the television reporter from Channel 8 kept on talking, "The Court Reporter for the Grand Jury, Allison Smith, has, for some mysterious reason, been shot at twice but both times the shooter missed. We can all be thankful for that. Much to everyone's relief, she will be okay. She has no apparent wounds of any kind. The police are frantically looking for the shooter."

Pagglione was fit to be tied. He was thinking: I have been upstaged by that witch, but if I play my cards right nothing will come of it. Who would ever suspect me? His eyes glowed as he looked around. He snickered to himself and plotted his next move.

The thought of McCallister and Summers being up to their necks in the murderous scheme and being in as much danger of getting caught as himself never entered his mind. He was concerned about one person, himself. Being involved in an undercover criminal activity in the past, Pagglione has expertise at covering his tracks.

Although he is very disappointed in the outcome, he thought: All I need to do is carry on, as usual; be the professional District Attorney that everyone thinks I am. Play the part to the hilt. It will be just a matter of time and it will be long forgotten.

I'm so angry at Dino. If I ever see his mug again, I will tear into him. How in the hell did he screw up? Professional hit man. I question that. Stupid, more like it. Pagglione ranted and raved to himself, all the time trying to get control of his emotions so that he could go on the air and make a statement.

All the way to the Denver International Airport, Dino was replaying the moment of failure in his brain. He is tense, but he knew the minute he got out of the country he would relax and begin to enjoy life again, but not like when he returned from all of his other murderous crusades. I'm short a million bucks which will put me back a bit. It will damn sure put a damper on my lifestyle. He dwelled on his money problems until he arrived at the airport.

A guy named Freddy was there to pick up the Bronco, just like clockwork. Dino, looking satisfied, never did miss a beat as to plan ahead, to be prepared if and when he had to escape, whenever things might go wrong.

When he stepped inside the airport terminal, he immediately went to the restroom and changed his clothes, putting on a silk suit, silk tie, and alligator shoes. He combed his hair in a slick style and stuffed his old clothes in an outside garbage container, way to the bottom.

Then he decided to have a few drinks. By the time he boarded his flight from Denver, he was flying high. When he arrived in New York, he boarded his flight within a couple of hours to Rome, Italy. He began to relax and enjoy himself and felt relieved to be headed for home.

Still, he said to himself: I can't stop thinking about the loss of a million bucks. I feel somewhat uneasy that maybe I could lose some business when the news leaks out that I made a mistake.

I know better than to wage a war with Pagglione. No use crying over spilled milk. As far as Dino is concerned, regarding Vinny, he grumbled: He is not any better than me. He just thinks he is. Vinny, in the future, get somebody else to do your dirty work.

Everyone became so involved with Allison's well-being that no one noticed how quickly the sheriff and police officers responded. They immediately secured the scene in the courtroom, called for backup, and upon seeing the two bullet holes in the wall, no one could fathom something like this happening. No one could figure out why anyone would want to kill this lovely girl.

In the meantime, Allison arrived at the Hospital's Emergency Room.

CHAPTER 29

Meg was dying of curiosity, as she waited for the breaking news on television that night, specifically to see if there would be indictments handed down from the Grand Jury members. She felt strongly that it was a travesty of justice when good people in the community like Rita Clark and the videographers have to suffer in such a cruel way because of so much corruption by the District Attorneys and investigator.

Finally the news she was waiting for came on the air. Pagglione began smiling into the cameras as he proudly told the people in Denver that the Grand Jurors had made their decision to indict Rita Clark, John Barker and Sam Lucas, and rightfully so, began his comment.

Pagglione appeared to Meg to be grandstanding. Meg couldn't believe how much he looked like a crooked politician. After she watched and listened to Pagglione, she was not at all surprised how arrogant he is. Allison had never uttered a word about Pagglione to Meg, negative or otherwise.

Meg began listening to Pagglione, trying to figure out what made him tick, when lo and behold Allie appeared on the television screen. Meg put her hands over her face in disbelief, but when she heard Allie scream, "Somebody tried to kill me," every nerve in her body collapsed. When Meg came to the realization that someone had tried to kill Allison, she was relieved to hear that she was not hurt. Meg shouted. "She is alive. I'm so thankful. I feel such joy." The broadcaster said that the ambulance had arrived and told the viewers that she was being taken to Lutheran Hospital.

Meg thought out loud. I have to call Allison's family and Sarah. I need to get to the hospital as soon as I can. It is extremely difficult to make these calls. Everyone will be shocked, but knowing that Allie is safe and has no injuries will help to relieve their concerns. Meg called and talked to Allison's father, and he couldn't believe anyone in this world would want to harm their Allie. No one could.

Allison's father, after relaying the information to the family, immediately called the airlines to check available flights to Denver. Meg called Sarah and tried to break it to her gently.

"Sarah, hi. This is Meg. I'm sure you are surprised I'm calling you. It's about Allie."

"She is alright, isn't she?"

Meg tried to speak calmly. "Yes. She's going to be fine. I don't know quite how to say it because it hasn't even registered with me, but someone tried to kill her."

"What? You have got to be kidding?"

"No, Sarah I'm not kidding. I don't even have any details yet. She was taken by ambulance to the Lutheran Hospital. I saw Allie on television. She came running out of the courthouse and screamed, 'Someone is trying to kill me.' I was stunned, Sarah. I've talked to her father. They are flying to Denver as soon as possible."

"Meg. It is shocking news, but thank the Lord she is alive. I can't believe it."

"Well, Sarah, you are right. We can all be grateful that she's alive. I will let you know what is going on as soon as I find out. I'm on my way to see her at the hospital. Take care."

"Meg, give her my love. I'll get there as soon as I can get a flight out."

"I know she will want her family and you by her side, Sarah. Talk to you later."

When Sarah hung up the phone, she was visibly shaken. Her thoughts turned to Todd. I am not sure what to do. Should I call Todd and tell him? I do feel compassion for him. It would be cruel on my part not to let him know what has happened.

Allie may hate me for doing this, but I'm going to call him. Sarah picked up the phone and dialed Todd's number.

"Hello."

"Hi Todd. This is Sarah. Are you sitting down?"

"No. Why? Laughingly Todd began to tease Sarah. "Hey, I thought you were not speaking to me anymore."

"Todd, this is serious. I don't like to be the bearer of bad news, but someone tried to kill Allie. I don't have any of the details, but Allie ended up on television. Meg told me Allie ran out of the courthouse screaming, 'Someone tried to kill me.' Then she collapsed."

Todd began experiencing a meltdown. "Sarah, tell me it is not true."

"Yes, it happened. Meg saw it live on the Denver local news."

"Who in the world would want to kill Allie? I can't believe what you are telling me. My heart is racing. Sarah, I still deeply love her."

"I know you do. That's why I'm telling you. I truly couldn't, in good conscience, not call you and let you know. Todd, I'll keep you up-to-date regarding how she is doing. I'm trying to get a flight out as soon as I wrap up some business. Love you Todd. I'll call you soon."

"Sarah, love you too. You do not know how much I appreciate your thoughtfulness in thinking of me. You are the best, you know that? One question before you go. What hospital is she in?"

"Lutheran. Take care."

Todd hung up the phone and immediately called the florist and ordered a dozen long stemmed red roses. Then, without another thought, he called the airlines.

When Allison arrived at the Emergency Room, her vital signs were immediately checked. She had some preliminary tests run, showing that she was suffering from malnutrition and mild dehydration. The doctor immediately ordered bed rest for two days with more tests to be taken.

When Meg arrived, the Front Desk said that no visitors would be allowed into Allison Smith's room except immediate family. Meg felt upset, but understood, and gave the receptionist a message to be given to Allison and then left the hospital.

The detectives and news media were waiting to communicate with Allison, but the doctors told them that she would be unable to talk to them for at least two days.

When I awoke early in the morning, looking around and realizing I was in a hospital bed, I could not help but stare at a vase filled with a dozen beautiful red roses, my favorite. I read the card out loud: "To My One and Only Love," signed Todd Lewis.

I can't believe it. I smiled and the tears started flowing. It is difficult to describe how I feel. It is overwhelming.

In the meantime, Todd arrived at the Denver International Airport at 6:30 a.m., the following morning, rented a car, and drove to the Lutheran Hospital in Lakewood. His thoughts were mingled with frustration but at the same time, hope.

Will she accept my apology? Will she forgive me? I wonder if by some miracle she still loves me? Why would she? I acted so brainless in not being honest with Allie.

I felt so pressured and fearful that I couldn't bring myself to go to her and tell her the truth. No matter what, I'm still going to give it a try. I'm scared to death she will reject me. Oh, well. I'll never be able to forgive myself if I don't tell her how I really feel. I love her from the bottom of my heart. There will never be anyone for me but Allie. She has impeccable character which makes her beautiful in my eyes.

Todd arrived at Lutheran Hospital, slipped in quietly and found out Allison's room number, telling the receptionist he was

Allison's brother. He lied. He thought to himself: I will have to repent later.

Allison had just spoken with the doctor who told her she needed be sure to rest, and he put her on a high nutrition diet. She was alone in the room when Todd slipped in. He took one look at her and broke into tears.

I am shocked to see Todd standing there with tears flowing. "Todd, what are you doing here?"

"Oh, Allie, I had to see you. I'm so very sorry for everything. Can I kiss you on the forehead?"

I am dumbfounded. I am genuinely happy for the first time in a long time. "Of course you can, you devil." Actually, I am concerned about Todd. He looks way too thin and totally worn out.

"Allie, for the life of me, I can't believe anyone would want to kill you. That just blows me away."

"It's a long story. Let's talk about that later, okay?"

"Okay, Allie."

"Todd, thank you for the beautiful red roses. You remembered that roses are my favorite flower. You know just what makes a girl happy."

"Allie, I have missed you more than you will ever know."

"To be honest, I have missed you too, Todd. By the way, how did you know I was here? Do I need to ask? Sarah?"

"Uh-huh." Todd attempted to look innocent.

"Well, if she went behind my back in calling you, then I'll have to go behind her back and tell you that I know all about Molly Jo. Sarah told me everything."

"Allie, I was so wrong in not telling you the truth and being sneaky. I know it is a cheap excuse, but I was feeling a lot of pressure from my parents. I'm not on very good terms with them even now."

"Todd Lewis, let's get something straight right off the bat. They are your parents, and maybe at that time they felt this girl, Molly Jo, was best for you. You know as well as I do that you have to repent and forgive them. The Savior has taught us how important it is to repent and forgive, and after all your parents are wonderful people, and they love you very much.

I forgive your mother and father, although I was heartbroken to think they cared more for Molly Jo than me. I thought they loved me a lot, and when I realized they didn't, it hurt me deeply."

"Well, Allie, we all learn from our mistakes, and I think before it was all over between Molly Jo and me, they realized how much they did love you and they know in their hearts they interfered way too much. It has strained our relationship a great deal."

"Todd, I have never known you to carry bad feelings toward anybody very long. Your first step is to repent and tell them how much you love them. You know as well as I do that love makes the world go around and keeps us spiritually grounded. The Savior teaches us that."

"Now I know why I have always loved you so much. You are so understanding, Allie, and still as beautiful as ever.

I am not sure that this is the appropriate time to talk about this, but I might as well tell you that my life has been one roller coaster after another since I returned from my mission. I have felt so empty inside without you. It has been difficult to move forward."

Tears streamed down my face. "Todd, I have missed you more than words can express. I love you so very much too. You were my anchor. When I lost you, Todd, I had to move forward, but I was uncertain as to how I could ever get along without you. I'm not lying when I tell you it has been a difficult road."

At that point, a nurse peeked her head in the door and ordered Todd to leave. Todd hugged me tight and kissed me tenderly. He told me he would see me first thing in the morning. His face was flushed when he left the room.

Todd skipped down the hall and laughed to himself. I feel like I'm on Cloud Nine. With luck on my side, he thought, I'm wasting no time. I'm heading for the jewelry store. I know exactly the ring that Allie would want, simple but exquisite.

Todd got in the rental car and said a silent prayer. Throughout his ordeal, he never forgot to call upon his Heavenly Father. He prayed often.

Throughout the morning I talked to my family. They are so distraught. What a great feeling to feel so loved. I tried to explain things, which was virtually impossible. I did not mention that Todd was by my bedside earlier. I wanted to wait until they were present. I wanted to surprise them.

By afternoon Sarah was able to get hold of Allie. Sarah is frantic.

"Allie, I finally am able to talk to you. I do not want to wear you out, but I am anxious to hear your voice. Allie, thank the Lord you are alive."

"Sarah. Hi. I am going to survive. Hey, Sarah, what have you been up to? Todd sent me a dozen red roses and was here in person, at my bedside, this morning. I am so happy that it is difficult to be mad at you. You are a stinker, Sarah."

"Oh, Allie. Are you kidding me? I didn't know he was going to fly to Denver to be with you. Oh my gosh, he got there before us. Are you angry with me?"

Sarah tried to sound calm, but in reality she was a bundle of nerves.

"Heavens, no. I owe you a lot Sarah. You did the right thing, but I wouldn't have been able to say that until now. In fact, even though I have been through such a nightmare, still, I haven't been this content for a very long time." I laughed as I spoke. "Admittedly, Sarah, because you went behind my back, I decided I could tell Todd that you told me everything about his relationship with Molly Jo."

"Well, Allie, the most important thing is that you are grateful I told Todd and not angry with me. Still, I'm not believing that anyone would want to kill you. I suppose there was a lot going on behind the scenes that you never told any of us about."

"Sarah, I will never be able to tell you everything. We are under an Oath of Secrecy in the Grand Jury. So, I will not ever be able to divulge a lot of what has happened to me."

"Well, Allie, I understand. I want you to rest. Before I go, I want you to know that if anything would have happened to you, I don't know what I would have done. I've leaned on you and your family so much in my life, and I would be lost without you."

"Sarah, you are a dear friend, someone I know I can always count on to be there for me. That's a great feeling. I love you. Take care."

"I love you too, Allie. I'll see you soon. You take care."

I feel so grateful for so many things, the gospel, family, and friends. I know within my heart that the Lord has protected me. I am still alive, and I want to shout for joy. An overwhelming feeling of love towards the Savior engulfs me. I prayed with thankfulness in my heart.

My thoughts are mixed as I analyze the situation I am facing. Everything seems so surreal and crazy, and, yet, I know my rights and I refuse, at this time anyway, to speak to any of those bloodthirsty maniacs. I need some time to think this over.

I'm probably going to have to hire a lawyer before all is said and done.

After the attempted murder of Allison, a Search Warrant was granted to go into her townhome. The detectives were looking for evidence but found nothing. Someone got there before they did.

Allison kept her journal in the bottom drawer of the nightstand in her bedroom. The journal told all, every minute detail on a day-to-day basis; the fear; the nightmares; the sleepless nights; the off-the-record discussions going on between the Grand Jurors and Pagglione, McCallister, and Summers; the way Judge Zacharelli treated her; how he had threatened her; how they had mocked Rita Clark's attorney, Sinclair Bennett, and tried to make the Grand Jurors think he was dumber than dumb; and worst of all, changing words on the original transcripts.

One of Pagglione's hired crooks broke into Allison's townhome right at the time Dino was attempting to kill her. He stole all the evidence. Pagglione ended up with all the evidence. He put it in a safe. The journal was his prized possession. He commented to himself: This will be a fun read. Then he laughed hysterically.

At the same time, Pagglione, McCallister, and Summers didn't waste any time in getting together to shred every confidential document they had pertaining to the Rita Clark case.

The community was demanding answers about the attempted murder of Allison Smith. People were outraged that the courthouse wasn't more secure. Judge Zacharelli was infuriated with Pagglione.

He was tormented, and he murmured: I know well enough to let everything die down a bit, but when I see Pagglione I'm going to give him a piece of my mind. I would like to knock him alongside of the head is what I'd like to do. I'd also like to know what he was thinking when he made plans to murder the girl right in the courthouse. I thought he had more brains than that. Couldn't he have figured out a better location than that? He is a buffoon.

I will have to keep my distance from Vinny for a time. I'll have to proceed with caution myself.

I am positive of one thing and that is Pagglione will never rat on me. I know too much of his past. I'm not certain about Allison Smith and wonder if she will try to involve me in the whole mess. I'm tense and full of anxiety. I hope Allison Smith keeps her mouth shut. If she doesn't, she'll pay a heavy price.

Todd, in the meantime, found the perfect engagement ring for Allie. His heart is full of hope. He thought to himself: I know she will like it. The big question is, will she accept it? Right now I'm sweating blood. Please, Allie, do not turn me down. Please forgive me.

Todd's plan is to return to the hospital the next morning early before the family arrive from Utah. His main goal is to pop the question. He can hardly contain his excitement.

A beautiful sunrise greeted Todd when he awoke early the next morning. He is wanting to look his best when he proposes to Allison. He is wearing his favorite pair of slacks and a red sweater that Allison bought him one year for Christmas. He slipped the ring in his sock.

Allison is thinking: A hospital is not the best place to get adequate rest. I was awake several times during the night.

There is so much going on. I can hardly believe it. I cannot believe that Todd is here with me. I am so in love with Todd and always have been. My mind is flitting from one thought to another.

I have never been happier in my life to see Todd and hold him near to me, but, on the other hand, I'm frightened to death that someone is wanting to kill me and seriously question that the man in black will attempt to kill me again.

There is no question in my mind as to why they are after me. I know too much. I am a witness to all the criminal activity that has been going on in the Grand Jury case. It is frightening to think about the horrific situation I find myself involved in through no choice of my own.

Todd slipped into the hospital early in the morning. When he arrived at the door of Allison's room, he was shaking. He said a short prayer, asking Heavenly Father to help him find the right words to convey his love and desire to marry Allison.

Todd stepped into the room with a great big smile on his face.

"Hi Allie. Up early. How did you sleep?" He gave her a tender kiss on the forehead and hugged her gently with feelings of deep love in his heart. He then began to sweat.

"Hi, Todd. I didn't expect to see you at sunrise. I'm so glad you are here with me. You look mighty handsome this morning. Now, what are you up to Todd Lewis?" I always enjoyed teasing him.

"Allie. Be serious. First of all, I need to tell you, I love you more than words can express. I have missed you more than I ever imagined I would. You are my sweetheart, and I truly mean it, Allie, when I say I can't live without you."

"Todd, what are you trying to say?"

"Allie, I do not want to take the chance of losing you again. With all my heart I want you to go to the temple with me to be married for time and all eternity. It is difficult to put into words how much I love you Allie. What is your answer?

I giggled with delight and said, "Yes. Yes, I will. I love you too, Todd Lewis. I can't believe that my dream has come true."

"Allie, I hope you like the ring I bought you yesterday."

Todd removed the velvet box from his sock and handed it to Allie and said in an excited tone, "I was so afraid you would turn me down. I don't know what I would have done if you would have rejected me."

"Oh, Todd, the ring is gorgeous. My, you have good taste. I would have picked this ring out for myself. You are so wonderful. Thank you for being so sweet and thoughtful. Of course, Todd Lewis, that's why I fell in love with you in the first place. That's why I could not forget you, try as I may. You are everything I always wanted."

We embraced for several minutes with tears streaming down our faces. "Todd, I feel happier than I have been for such a long time, but I am still apprehensive about my dangerous situation. Todd, what about the fact that someone is trying to kill me? Doesn't that bother you? Your own life could be in jeopardy just by being with me."

"Allie, wherever you are, I will be with you and do everything in my power to protect you."

"The next time they may not make a mistake. My life could end."

"We will fight back, Allie. We need to have faith that all will turn out well."

I leaned on Todd's shoulder. "Allie, let's start out right and pray. We need to thank our Heavenly Father for bringing us together again. Let's promise each other that we will stay attuned to the spirit and follow the path of our Savior as best we can. If we live righteously, we will receive the comfort and guidance we are going to need in the future."

They knelt by the bedside, and Todd gave a beautiful prayer straight from his heart. Then they hugged each other tight and kissed tenderly.

"Oh, Todd, it is so wonderful to be alive and to be with you. It is more than I dreamed of. It's overwhelming.

Seriously, Todd, there is one thing you need to know. I took an Oath of Secrecy when I was sworn in to be the Grand Jury Reporter. So I can't talk about what has transpired. I may never be able to tell you what happened in all truthfulness. An investigation will go forward and then everything will be disclosed to the proper authorities. At this point we have to be patient and take one day at a time. I need an attorney that I can trust to advise me on how to proceed."

"Allie, whatever you have to do, I will support you in every way I possibly can. Let's now enjoy our time being with each other. Both of us need to depend on our Savior to help us along the way."

"Todd, I've been depending on our Savior ever since I was a little girl. There is no way I could have gone through this terrible ordeal without the Savior." They embraced for the longest time and kissed each other passionately.

"Changing the subject, but my family and Sarah will be coming in today. Won't they be surprised? We need to celebrate our engagement and, of course, Lydia's new baby boy. I wonder what Mother and Daddy will say." I giggled. "They will be so thrilled to see you. They will also be thrilled to see us together. Todd, Mother and Daddy love you so much. They never used harsh words against you, but they saw how depressed I was, and they were terribly hurt."

"I know, Allie. Do you think they can find it in their hearts to forgive me? It scares me. I was so afraid to approach you or your parents that I stayed away but suffered from unbelievable guilt."

"Bless you. Mother and Daddy are not the kind of people that hold grudges. Watch and see.

Sweetheart, I need you to do me a big favor."

"I am at your service."

"Thank you, Todd. Grab my purse and get the keys to my condo. Here is the address. By the way, I want you to stay there with me for as long as you want to. It's not that far from the hospital. You'll find it very cozy."

"Thank you, Allie. You are still as generous as you used to be."

"This is important, Todd. In the bottom drawer of my nightstand is my journal. If you would bring that to me as well as my computer, I would appreciate it. I know I can trust you not to read anything in my journal or anything that is on my computer. Okay?"

"Sure, Allie. Do you want me to go get your journal and computer now?"

"Yes, please, if you would, the sooner the better."

When Todd arrived at Allison's condo, he did not find her journal in the nightstand. He looked high and low for her journal and computer. Neither was to be found. Todd was upset. Someone has broken into Allie's place and stolen evidence. When I return to the hospital empty-handed, I wonder what Allie's reaction will be. She will be devastated.

When Todd returned to the hospital, he immediately entered her room and said, "Allie, I'm sorry but your journal and computer are not there. I scoured your place. You have been robbed."

"Todd, I feel sick to my stomach. Oh, Todd, I was counting on the journal to back up evidence of the criminal activity that took place during the Grand Jury sessions. I don't dare say anything more than that."

"Babes, don't take it too seriously. It will all work out. Your family will be here very soon. We all need to celebrate your being alive and, most importantly, that we are going to get married. Let's take one step at a time."

Todd is worried. I don't want to alarm Allie any more than she already is. She has experienced a great deal of trauma, and I do worry about her safety.

"Todd, I will need time to do my own investigating. That way I will be able to discover who I can trust. I am not going to lie to you. The situation is scary. I am dealing with monsters."

"Yes, Allie. Take your time. I'll help you in any way I can. You are not alone. I love you deeply."

"The feeling is mutual, Todd."

CHAPTER 30

Allison's mother and dad and Sarah arrived in Denver on the same flight. Allison's father insisted on paying for Sarah's ticket. Upon arrival at the hospital, the three of them felt a great deal of excitement as they entered Allison's room. Immediately upon entering the room, there is an abundance of love and happiness.

I am thrilled to see mother and daddy and Sarah. It is impossible to describe the joyous reunion, especially with Todd present. When I showed the ring to my family and Sarah, we all cried for the joy we were feeling.

"Oh, Todd," Allison's mother spoke with humility. "This is so unexpected, but how happy we are for the both of you. It's so great to see you. We have missed your smiling face young man. Let bygones be bygones, and may you and Allie cherish each other forever."

Todd gave Sister Smith a big bear hug and said, "Thank you, Sister Smith, for accepting me with love in your hearts. Brother Smith, I was so afraid to approach   you and ask you if I could marry your daughter after how I had behaved that I just put the situation in the Lord's hands, and then I did what I felt I had to do. I love your daughter from the bottom of my heart."

"Allie's mother and I always loved you, Todd. Of course, we were heartbroken when you didn't contact any of us, but that's over now."

The hospital had a security guard outside Allison's room from the time she was admitted. The family couldn't believe what Allie had been experiencing without them ever knowing.

Inasmuch as they were only there for a couple of days, they did not want to ruin the precious time they had to spend with Todd and Allison. So they collectively decided not to ask too many questions that would upset them.

Sarah lovingly held Allie's hand and said, "Allie, thank the Lord you are alive." Then she broke down in tears.

Brother Smith smiled broadly. "We are just happy that you are alive, Allie. We know with our Heavenly Father's help all will end well. We wish you all the happiness in the future.

Brother Smith looked affectionately at Sarah and said, "Sarah, we want you to be with us while we are here in Denver celebrating. Let us pray."

My loved ones knelt by my bedside. Daddy gave the most beautiful prayer imaginable, thanking our Heavenly Father for my life being spared and for all of our blessings.

CHAPTER 31

Pagglione cooperated with the investigators in every way. He tried to remain as calm as possible. He had only one mindset. He kept saying to himself: I'm going to take some time off. I want to go to Hawaii or somewhere where I won't be disturbed, but common sense tells me that I will have to wait until things cool down a bit. I need to give serious consideration as to what my next move should be.

The biggest relief to me is that Allison is refusing to speak to anyone at the   moment. This makes me think that she is still fearful. What a stroke of luck. I still have to deal with Summers and McCallister. Allison may feel fearful enough that she may never come forward. I can hope for that.

At first Pagglione, Summers, and McCallister held their breaths knowing they were going to have to do some quick thinking if and when the time came to prove themselves innocent of any wrongdoing. None of them felt that Allison had a leg to stand on. With a quick move on their part, they had destroyed all of the evidence.

Pagglione thought: I am going to have myself one hell of a good time once this blows over. Let's face it, if Allison tries to tell anything now, most people will think she is crazy, or I will make sure they think it. They would question why she didn't come forward and tell what was going on way before now. I'm convinced that the jurors have no suspicions whatsoever of anything being out of the ordinary.

Having Allison's journal and computer wipes away the crucial evidence.

I'm hearing from the rumor mill, most of the jurors think I did an excellent job in presenting the case, and that they are extremely impressed by my professionalism.

McCallister and Summers seem to be loosening up a bit, and they too are impressed with my handling of this awkward situation. They understand that I am a leader. I took the bull by the horn and have kept all of them out of hot water. I'm their man, and they know it.

Dino arrived in Rome feeling as cocky as always. A family limo was waiting to drive him south to Naples, and then he was planning on sailing to the Isle of Capri on his family's private yacht.

Dino stretched and shouted: "Finally I'm back on safe turf. The fresh air exhilarates me. Good to be home. It feels great."

Rosie was going to wait for six months and then resign from her library job in Arvada. She then planned to also go home to the Isle of Capri. She told herself that even though she was disappointed with the outcome of Dino not being able to kill Allison Smith, she knew Dino would shake it off and be out there making millions on a new deal in no time. She also knew she would get a hefty sum even though they didn't pull it off.

Things have turned out just dandy as far as she is concerned. She was assured that she was in the clear. In fact, she told Dino that she had the time of her life being a member of the Grand Jury. She did complain that she missed the material life, especially being able to wear her diamonds. She is anxious to get back home and live it up. She wants to celebrate nonstop when it comes time for her homecoming, and why not?

She made up her mind to explore some of the beautiful areas of Colorado on the weekends, knowing she would never return once she leaves.

Dino vowed not to take another job for a year. His mafia family said they would help him out financially so that he could continue to live in the style he was accustomed to. He was given the choice to work or not work. It was entirely up to him.

The minute Dino's mafia friends knew he was on his way home, big time names were seeking out his services. It didn't take that long before he was in a position to pick and choose.

Pagglione was basking in the limelight. The radio and the newspapers were filled with articles about the Rita Clark case. Pagglione was being praised as one of the best District Attorneys in the State of Colorado. As days passed, Pagglione became more and more at ease, especially when there was no word from Allison Smith.

Pagglione kept telling himself: I am certain that the more she delays in speaking out, the better my chances are of coming up with a story that proves she is incompetent. It would be a good move on my part to make sure it gets in the newspapers. That will stop her in her tracks. .

I'll attack Allison Smith with a vengeance, especially if she opens her big mouth. I'll make sure that the public understands that she is a rather mediocre Court Reporter. Never in a million years will they suspect me now, nor McCallister or Summers.

Pagglione, McCallister and Summers, when they got together in private for a conference, told jokes, laughed at how easy they had gotten off scot-free, made more fun of Rita Clark, Sinclair Bennett, Allison Smith, even some of the Grand Jurors, and John Barker and Sam Lucas.

After my parents and Sarah flew back to Utah, I was released from the hospital with a clean bill of health. Todd had just completed an internship as a clerk for a Federal Judge in Salt Lake. So he was free and willing to help me in every way he could.

One morning Todd said to me, "Allie, I am happy to be here with you. Our time together has been priceless. Come here and hold my hand. Lean on me. You've got more courage than most people I have ever known."

"Todd Lewis, I can't believe we are together. I feel your love and comfort. I never told you this before because I did not want you to get a big head, but from the moment I met you, it was love at first sight. Truly, I feel safe with you. Let me hug you tightly. I'll never ever let you go."

"I do not remember feeling so great, Allie. I adore you and always have."

A week passed since I was nearly killed. While Todd and I were sitting on the deck laughing about old times, the phone rang.

"Todd, I better answer it."

"Hello. This is Vincent Pagglione."

I immediately froze: He didn't even ask me how I am getting along. Of course not. I'll bet he is extremely annoyed that I'm not dead.

"Hi, Vincent." I told myself to remain calm. I looked at Todd and gestured for him not to say a word.

Pagglione grinned wickedly. "Allison, I will be brief. This is very important. You need to meet with me and Judge Zacharelli Saturday morning in his chambers, promptly at 10:00 a.m." The Judge did not want anyone to be able to contact Allison before he talked to her. "Got that?"

My voice is shaky. "Yes."

Pagglione hung up abruptly and thought, Man, I'm glad Nick got me off the hook on this one.

Todd held Allie tightly. "Todd, I feel scared. I have to meet with Judge Zacharelli on Saturday morning. Thank goodness you are here. Thank you for staying with me through this horrendous ordeal. You are so patient and understanding with me. I am blessed beyond words."

"Babes, I understand that you have been under an enormous amount of pressure. I'm behind you all the way. I love you. I'll drive you to the courthouse on Saturday and wait for you in the car. Don't worry. It's best that we pray and have faith. Everything will turn out just fine. Come over here close to me. Let me give you hugs and kisses. You are such a wonderful girl."

"Todd, I love you too. I have been on my own for so long that I can't tell you what it means to have you by my side. The Lord is ever mindful of our needs."

"Babes, I thank the Lord for giving me a second chance to be with you. It blows my mind to think that, after all this time, we will be together, married in the House of the Lord for time and all eternity. Let us pray." They knelt in fervent prayer and wept.

"Thank you, Todd, for that beautiful prayer. You know, depending on the Lord and prayer and the reading of the scriptures is the only reason I have been able to survive. Now, I'm so gloriously happy at this moment with the knowledge that I will have the power of the priesthood in my home, and I need to pinch myself at the realization that you are actually here with me."

Pagglione is a broken record by his constant muttering: I'm anxious to get these matters settled so I can get out of town and celebrate. Hawaii sounds so fun right now. I'm sick to death of the Judge breathing down my neck. He has such a demanding way about him.

The following day the Judge and Pagglione are scheduled to meet each other privately in the Judge's chambers. They do an outstanding job of pretending to like each other. The Judge, for many reasons, is so disappointed in Pagglione.

The Judge keeps saying over and over in his mind: Vinny is such an arrogant buffoon. I can't count on him to handle anything right.

When Vincent steps into the Judge's chambers ten minutes early, the mood changes instantly. They are telling jokes and laughing.

"Vinny, let's get down to business now. What do you think our next move should be regarding Allison?"

"Judge, the only thing we can do is fire her. The thought of seeing her again is disturbing. She is not what we expected."

"I agree with you wholeheartedly, Vinny. She is more trouble than she is worth at this point."

Saturday came too quickly for me. Todd drove me to the courthouse.

Before I stepped out of the car, Todd gave me a big hug and kissed me.

"Honey, I'm sure this won't take too long. You stay put. I don't want you harmed in any way. I will be fine, no matter what the outcome. I'm scared to death, but these feelings have been ongoing for so long, I think I should have built up an immunity be now."

"I love you, Allie."

"I love you too."

The Judge and Pagglione were sitting across from each other waiting for Allison to arrive. The Judge, in his boisterous voice said, "I never did like that Allison Smith that much. I think we definitely made the wrong choice."

Vincent laughed. "We did at that. All I can say is, she better keep her mouth shut."

"Vinny, we have got to act compassionate towards Allison regarding what happened to her. Still, I'm going to scare the daylights out of her."

Vincent had a devilish smile on his face when Allison Smith appeared at the entrance to Judge Zacharelli's chambers promptly at five minutes to ten. The Judge sat comfortably in his high-back leather chair.

I looked at Vincent Pagglione with that wicked expression on his face. If looks could kill, I would be dead. My heart is pounding. Oh, no. Evil lurks.

"Hi Allison. Come on in and have a seat."

"Good morning Judge and Vincent."

"Hi Allison."

I thought to myself: The Judge and Vincent are involved in this corruption right up to their necks. They are a bunch of crooks. I've got to remain calm. "

It took effort for the Judge to be civil. "How are you getting along? Sorry about your traumatic experience. You can't trust anybody anymore. We understood that you could only have family visiting at the hospital. So we stayed away."

Vincent had to put his two cents worth in. "Sorry as well. Unfortunately, there are a lot of kooks and nuts running around out there."

I couldn't help but think: Both of you should include yourselves in that category. I know you could care less about me. So go ahead and pretend. No matter what you say, be polite, Allie. "Yes, it was a traumatic experience. I'm getting along much better. Thank you for asking."

"Well, Allison, the Judge said, "I'll get right to the point. I have a meeting I have to attend. The last transcript you delivered was not satisfactory. It was full of errors. After discussing it with Vinny, we both came to the decision that we have no other choice but to terminate you.

Also, I would like to reiterate what we have already talked about before. Do not take lightly the Secrecy Oath that you took as the Grand Jury Reporter. You can go to jail if you divulge any information that goes on in the Grand Jury proceedings. I know you understand."

Pagglione spoke to me in a rude manner. "Just so you are clear, Allison, the Grand Jury Contract reads that it is at our discretion to fire a Court Reporter if and when we find it necessary and, of course, in this situation it's the only avenue we feel we can take."

I am dumbfounded. I feel my face turning red, and at the same time I am completely brokenhearted. I have never had one complaint from any judge or lawyer that my transcripts were full of errors. All I have received have been compliments. In fact, I have been accused of being a perfectionist.

"Full of errors" is such a horrendous lie. They are rotten to the core. I have been the Grand Jury Reporter for six years now, working on unbelievable deadlines, doing all that was asked of me, even putting myself in a dangerous situation by changing the words on transcripts, and what do I get? I was holding back the tears.

The Judge stood and said, "You are excused. Good luck to you in the future." Tears began to fall and I was utterly speechless. I left the Judge's chambers fuming. I couldn't even bear to look at the two of them as I was leaving.

When Allison was no longer present, Pagglione chuckled. "Mission accomplished." He gave the Judge a slap on the back. "Hey Judge, what about a round of golf? After that, let's treat ourselves to drinks and a delicious steak."

"That sounds great to me, Vinny. I am glad that is over with. I need to make a few phone calls, and then I will meet you out at the Country Club."

CHAPTER 32

When I got to the car, I was sobbing. Todd took me in his arms and held me tightly. "Todd, I was fired. They said my transcripts were full of errors, and that they had no other recourse but to fire me. It was absolutely awful. Todd, they are big fat liars. They are wicked to the core."

"Honey, I'm so sorry. They are wicked. Don't worry."

Todd shows me so much love and comforts me with words of wisdom. "Babes, on a scale of one to ten, it's certainly not worth ruining our lives over. When we get to your condo, let's change our clothes and go up Waterton Canyon for a hike. You need to try to relax. How does that sound?"

"Anything to help me get rid of these scary feelings. I will say it over and over again, I can't imagine what I would have done if you wouldn't have been here with me. I have to thank Sarah for your presence. I, more than likely, would have gone to my condo and literally gone to bed and slipped into a deep depression."

"Allie, after the hike and we eat something very nutritious, hopefully that will help you to have a restful night, and then in the morning we'll talk about what is really important, our future. Okay?"

"Okay." I smiled at Todd lovingly. "Todd, you always used to plan such fun things for us to do. You are still spontaneous. I thought a lot about those great times we had together."

"Allie, I keep repeating myself, but I never thought that this day would ever come. I never fathomed that we would be together again."

"Well, I dreamed there was a possibility, and I prayed about it a lot."

On the way home I kept replaying over and over in her mind: Why didn't I tell someone about what was happening from the beginning, at the time the D.A.'s were going off the record and demanding that I make changes? I'm afraid I've waited until it's too late. Who would believe me now? They would think that I was lying, especially since Zacharelli has fired me. I can hear it all now. Allison Smith has been fired as the Grand Jury Court Reporter due to incompetency. On top of that they will say my transcripts are full of errors. Oh, my stomach is churning. Then they would accuse me of making up the most ridiculous accusations against the District Attorneys, Pagglione and McCallister.

"Todd, I hate to get you mixed up in all of this, but at the same time I'm so thrilled you are with me again. I feel sad and happy at the same time. It's like a miracle."

Todd beamed from ear to ear. "Allie, you make me so happy."

"I'm looking forward to what you have in mind for our future, Todd. Whatever it is, I have my honey back with me. Just think, I'm going to be your wife, your eternal wife. I'm so excited."

"You will never know how anxious I am to move on with you at my side. I think you'll like what I have in mind, Allie. I know how adventurous you are. Knowing you as well as I do, I am confident you will go along with my plans.

CHAPTER 33

The next morning Todd came into Allie's bedroom and shouted, "Rise and shine beautiful. Breakfast is ready and then we need to talk."

"It must be important." I giggled with anticipation. "First of all, Allie, how did you sleep?"

"Like a baby. Thank you for asking. I think it is because you are here. Truthfully, Todd, if you weren't here, it would have been a disaster for me. Since you have been here, even under these frightening circumstances, I have felt more secure. I love you, Todd Lewis."

Todd kissed Allison and said, "I love you too."

We sat down for breakfast. "Todd, did you learn how to cook on your mission? These eggs are delicious and the sausage is scrumptious."

"I'm glad you are enjoying my expert cooking." Todd laughed out loud. "Mother began teaching me more about cooking the last year of high school. Come on babes, let's have another cup of tea and go sit on the deck."

"Sounds wonderful."

We sat close to each other on the love seat. Todd put his arms around my shoulders. He is a gentle soul and so affectionate. He began speaking in a very sincere tone of voice.

"Allie, I've been thinking."

"Oooh, that can be dangerous."

"Seriously, Allie. How would you feel about getting married soon? I was thinking around Thanksgiving. Dad could arrange to get a date for us to be married in the Salt Lake Temple, and then we could have a reception afterwards. Hear me out. Then you tell me what you think. I want you to be honest with me."

"Okay, Todd. I am all ears."

"We get married around Thanksgiving and have a reception. Then we fly back to Denver and spend some time in your condo and then fly back to Utah to spend Christmas with our families.

Here comes the next idea. I've been saving my money that I earned from clerking in the Federal District Court. I have always wanted to backpack through Europe. We could leave in January, and I could delay entering Law School until Fall. Sweetheart, are you interested in what I'm proposing?"

"Am I? Need you ask? Give me a few minutes, and I will be packed. Todd Lewis, here you go again. Always the adventurer. It's a good thing that I am."

"Wait a minute, Allie. At this point you are no longer the Grand Jury Court Reporter. I realize that I am throwing a lot at you at once, but would you consider closing down your freelance business, selling your condo and moving to Salt Lake due to the fact that I have been accepted to attend Law School at the University of Utah"?

"Moving home? Oh, Todd, that sounds so wonderful. To think that we would be close to our families gives me goose bumps. I have missed my family so much. I have missed Sarah a lot too."

"Be honest with me, Allie. Do you love me enough to agree with what I am asking you to do?"

"Yes, I love you enough to agree. I laughed when I said, "And, of course, I would love to backpack through Europe, especially with you. We will have the time of our lives together.

You know, Todd, that both of our mothers will help out with the reception. I know mother has always wanted me to wear her wedding dress. I've tried it on before, and it fits me perfectly. Besides, I want to honor her by wearing her wedding dress.

Honey, I couldn't have dreamt up what you have planned in my confused state of mind, but you are definitely a man for all seasons. You are my man. That's what you are."

"Allie, I am so excited that you will go along with my plans. Babes, where do you want to have our reception?"

"Todd, let's have it in Park City at The Lodge. We were planning to go there on a family vacation during Thanksgiving. How do you feel about that?"

"Whatever you want. That would be great."

The following morning, after breakfast, Todd walked over to the Drug Store to pick up a newspaper. Rita Clark's picture was splashed all over the front page. He began to read the article. Oh, no. Allie will flip. I have to read it again to believe it. "Allison Smith has been fired as the Grand Jury Court Reporter in

Jefferson County due to incompetence. Her transcripts were full of errors."

I don't want to show Allie this article, but I can't keep it from her either. How cruel can they get? I'm glad I've talked to Uncle George about Allie's horrendous situation.

Todd rushed to the condo with angry thoughts. She's been under so much pressure. Now, another blow. Allie is strong. She'll get through this with flying colors. The dust will eventually settle.

Todd walked into the living room of Allie's condo with a serious face.

"Hi Todd. What's the matter, honey? You look like you have seen a ghost."

"Worse. I picked up a newspaper. Allie, I didn't want you to see this, but you will find out sooner or later anyway. Here. I will let you read it for yourself."

I picked up the newspaper with fear in my heart. I began to read. "Oh, Todd. One devastating situation after another. I wish I'd never accepted being the Grand Jury Court Reporter. I have to be honest, I know the Judge well enough and the District Attorneys to believe this would happen and, sure enough, it has.

They are doing everything they can to destroy my reputation. I will have to bear up the best I can with your help." I broke down crying and feeling miserable.

"Honey, don't cry. I love you so much and will help you in every way that I can. Remember Uncle George?"

I am trying to pull myself together. "The short little baldheaded man?"

"Well, the little baldheaded man happens to be a brilliant attorney."

"I know that, Todd. I am not even aware of what I am saying. I didn't mean it in a derogatory way."

"I know that babes. You wouldn't harm a flea." Anyway, while you were busy talking to Sarah yesterday, I called him and told him everything I know. He suggested an excellent criminal attorney here in Denver who will see you. The man's name is Matthew McDonald. He's a member of the church.

You don't have to worry anymore about who you can trust and who you can't. You can tell him in detail what happened in the Grand Jury sessions and who you think is responsible for trying to kill you."

"Todd, I have heard of him, but our paths have never crossed. Yes. Thank you Todd for your concern. I thank the Lord that I can finally speak freely to someone that will understand.

"I knew you would agree, Allie. Your appointment is at 10 o'clock on Friday morning. So wipe your eyes and know that you will be in good hands."

"Todd Lewis, you are the best." We embraced each other. "I admire you and feel so much love for you right now."

CHAPTER 34

Matthew McDonald's offices are on the 17th Street Mall. Todd drove me to the high-rise building and dropped me off. "Babes, I will park the car and then I'll meet you in the reception area after you are finished. Good luck, sweetheart."

"Thank you so much." I threw Todd a kiss and felt blessed as I headed up 17th Street to the Brooks Building. Matthew McDonald's offices are on the top floor. When I got off the elevator, I stepped into a plush reception area. The receptionist introduced herself.

"Welcome. I am Karen. You must be Allison Smith?"

"Yes."

"Nice to meet you, Allison."

"Thank you. Very nice to meet you."

"Mr. McDonald is expecting you. Come with me, please."

When I entered Mr. McDonald's office, Karen said in a friendly tone, "Mr. McDonald, this is Allison Smith." My heart is beating fast. I feel stress.

"Good morning, Allison Smith. Do you want me to call you Allison? I know Uncle George referred to you as Allie."

"My friends call me Allie. You can call me Allie as well." I smiled at Mr. McDonald, and he gave me a warm smile. I began to unwind a bit.

"Well, Allie, you can call me Matthew. Before we get started, would you like something to drink?"

"Water will be fine. Thank you."

"Thank you Karen. That will be all for now."

"Okay, young lady. I'm going to take notes. So, please, go ahead and explain everything that took place in the Grand Jury sessions that were out of the ordinary, and then we will talk.

"I brought my own notes so I can refer to them. I do not want to miss anything important. I explained to Matthew, in detail, everything that had transpired that I felt involved criminal activity.

"Unfortunately, Matthew, my condo was broken into at the time this wicked creature was attempting to shoot me. Whoever it was took my journal and computer. My journal contained a day-to-day record of what was happening in my life, particularly what was happening in those Grand Jury sessions."

"One thing you can be assured of, Allie, is that when someone in authority, such as Vincent Pagglione, orders you to change words on transcripts or to go off the record, you are not responsible. You followed the instructions of the District Attorney who was the authority at that time. He is guilty as sin. You are free of any wrong-doing."

"Matthew, I have felt so trapped, and I couldn't figure out who I could turn to that I began to trust no one. I began to unravel. I still have anxiety, but less, because I have Todd in my life again."

"On a lighter note, Allie, congratulations. I couldn't help but notice that gorgeous diamond on your finger. Todd is a lucky guy."

I smiled. "Thank you so much. I am the lucky one."

"Where are you going to get married?"

"It's a dream come true. We are going to be married in the Salt Lake Temple in November, and then we will have a reception in Park City. For our honeymoon, we are going to backpack through Europe."

"Sounds wonderful. Okay, Allie, from what you have told me, most attorneys in this town wouldn't touch this case with a ten-foot pole. It's one of those devilish situations where there is no justice. Crooks stick together and look for scapegoats. You were the perfect candidate. They caught you off guard. I'm certain they are a bit shaken up, but at this point they are counting on you to keep your mouth shut.

They slandered you in the newspapers to hopefully create more fear in you. Know who you are. That's very important to your well-being. In other words, hold your head high. All I can say to comfort you is, you are not guilty of anything.

Move forward and live your life to the fullest. You'll look on this ghastly experience and wonder how you survived. The main thing is, you are a survivor.

My advice to you is to leave this whole ordeal behind you for now, but if and when you are ever ready to fight back, we will forge ahead. Believe you me, it will be a fight, but I am game if you are. Feel free to contact me at any time.

Right now, you have a bright future ahead of you. From what I can determine, it is going to be full of happiness."

"Thank you from the bottom of my heart, Matthew. You will be hearing from me in the future. I believe these crooks need to pay for their criminal activities. I will be contacting you in the future. You can count on it."

"May the Lord bless you and Todd and keep you safe from harm. Look back on this time as just a test and, remember, adversity makes us stronger so that we can weather the storms that come into our lives. The Savior is the best example we have of how important it is that we endure to the end."

CHAPTER 35

We could not have asked for a more beautiful wedding day. We arrived at the Salt Lake Temple feeling so excited and feeling so much in love. After we were married, we stood on the steps at the front of the Salt Lake Temple with all of our family and friends in attendance.

I threw my bouquet, and Sarah caught it. Tearfully we looked at each other. The love and strong bond of friendship that exists between us is written on our faces. Out of the corner of my eye, I noticed that Sarah was so thrilled.

Todd turned to me and whispered, "Allie, you are my beautiful bride. I feel blessed that we will be together for time and all eternity. I love you more than words can ever express."

We were both teary-eyed. I whispered, "Todd Lewis, you are handsome. I love you, honey. You are my knight in shining armor."

Then Todd grabbed me and gave me an unforgettable kiss.

Made in the USA
San Bernardino, CA
25 September 2015